FOSSIL
REVOLUTION

Collins

FOSSIL REVOLUTION

THE FINDS THAT CHANGED OUR VIEW OF THE PAST

Douglas Palmer

First published in 2003

Collins is an imprint of HarperCollinsPublishers Ltd.
77–85 Fulham Palace Road
London
W6 8JB

The Collins website address is:

www.collins.co.uk

08 07 06 05 04 03 02

10 9 8 7 6 5 4 3 2 1

Text © 2003 Douglas Palmer

ISBN 0 00 7118287

Edited and designed by Blackingstone Books

Colour reproduction by Saxon
Printed and bound by Bath Press

OPPOSITE:
A 570 million year old fossil embryo with its microscopic (berry-like) cluster of cells is uniquely preserved by phosphate minerals

PAGE 1:
Cretaceous Jaws – the ferocious jaws and teeth of a deep-water predatory mosasaur – Prognathodon salvayi

PAGE 2:
Amongst the first large organisms on Earth are these strange examples, unlike any living forms, which were found in Late Precambrian seabed sediments in Namibia, south-west Africa

PAGE 6–7:
Eichstaettisaurus schroederie of the Ardeosauridae family – considered to be related to the gecko family

Contents

Introduction

The discovery of fossils and their scientific meaning was a shocking business that radically altered our sense of ourselves and our relationship to other life forms. From thinking of ourselves as being one rung below the angels on the ladder to heaven, we have found that we are genetically over 98% chimp and just one of a dozen or more human-related species. At the next global Armageddon, bacteria, ants and rats probably stand a better chance of surviving and recovering more quickly than humans will. Such a dramatic and, for many, uncomfortable or even unacceptable change in status, has taken several hundred years to accomplish and a great deal of often very heated argument. How and why this transformation in our view of ourselves happened is the subject of this book.

Fossil remains of past life were first dug out of the rocks by our ancestors and relatives 100,000 years ago. We shall never know what these extinct fossil collectors, such as the Neanderthal people, thought of them. We do know that they attached some importance to fossils, because they deliberately incorporated them in some of their stone tools. Although an interest in collecting fossils and some concern with their nature is very ancient, we do not find any perceptible or particularly interesting change in attitude towards fossils until Classical times.

Since then, over the last three millennia, our sense of what fossils are, and what their existence signifies for our understanding of prehistory of the world, has been radically transformed. For the Classical world, fossils were seen as evidence for the existence of giant heroes and mythical animals. They were first transformed into evidence for the biblical Creation story and that of the Flood. Over the last 200 years or so they have been transformed again by the scientific revolution into something that is just as dramatic, much more complex, and much more interesting. This is the story of how life has diversified, been cut back by extinction events, and yet has recovered and continued to evolve.

My intention is to present a collection of true stories about this chronological trajectory of discovery, and the growing understanding of the life of the geological past. These stories of 'petrified life' (literally meaning 'life turned to stone') range from the 'far side' of life's prehistory, nearly 4,000 million years ago, when life consisted of little more than microbes squirming around in warm ponds, to recent prehistory and the discovery of our extinct human ancestors and relatives. However, the order in which the stories of different groups of animals and plants appear is dictated by their historical discovery rather than by their position in the biological hierarchy of life and its evolution. Invariably, common fossils and those that are remarkably large came to attention first. Interest in and the search for the earliest microbial evidence for life had to wait until biological theory was firmly established. And then there was a need for the right kind of experimental technique and equipment before such very small fossils could be studied, all of which did not really happen until the 1950s.

One might think that after 200 years of intensive search for fossils and their scientific study the pace of discovery and rate of recovery of really interesting specimens might be dropping off. Far from it. The last few years have seen some of the most remarkable finds and revelations, ranging from fluffy feathered dinosaurs to our earliest vertebrate ancestors dating back some 530 million years. There are two main reasons for this. Firstly, the known fossil record still only samples a very small percentage – far, far less than 1% – of the enormous diversity of life forms that have ever existed. Between several hundred million and a few thousand million species have existed over the last 540 million years (that part of the 4,600 million years of Earth history in which fossils are relatively common), of which only a few hundred thousand are known as fossil forms. Only a small percentage of organisms, mostly those with hard parts of some kind, can be fossilised. Even so, there are huge numbers of new and often exciting fossils still waiting to be dug out of the rocks.

Secondly, vast tracts of rock strata are still relatively unexplored. The history of discovery has largely focused on those terrains readily accessible to the majority of palaeontologists: initially Europe, then North America, Australia and parts of Africa and Asia. Now it is China, South America, Antarctica and so on. The finds from China over the last decade alone have revolutionised our understanding of the first vertebrates, of dinosaur and bird evolution, of early flowering plants and of the very early mammals.

Finally, we have to remember that our view of human prehistory is still at an early stage of discovery and understanding. We probably know more about the evolution of extinct groups of fossils, such as trilobites or dinosaurs, than we do about our own evolution.

Chapter 1

Stones, shells and sharks' teeth – early discoveries

First fossilists – the prehistoric discovery of fossils

Curiosity about fossils seems to be a particularly human attribute. There is no evidence that the chimps or any other higher apes are the least bit interested in them. However, as with so many human characteristics, there is an interesting question to be considered: when did this concern with fossils begin? Was it some 200,000 years ago with the evolution of the first modern humans, members of our species *Homo sapiens*, or did it begin even earlier with our extinct relatives such as the Neanderthals or perhaps the *Homo erectus* people who evolved 2 million or more years ago? Surprisingly, we do have evidence of a prehistoric interest in fossils from the archaeological record of stone tools.

Theoretically, since fossils are commonly found embedded in stone, their discovery could be as old as the first use of rock materials by our prehistoric ancestors. The earliest recognisable stone tools are 2.5 million years old and so the discovery of fossils might stretch back to that time, but I think it is unlikely to have been as long ago as this.

The reason for this is that the earliest stone tools, found in the Great Rift Valley of East Africa, are made of the most readily available and suitable local materials. These tend to be hard and brittle rocks, generally volcanic or a kind of quartz. None of these rocks is fossiliferous and so the process of

LEFT:
Some chimps use stone tools, but are unlikely to be interested in any fossils found in the stones. Our stone-tool-using human ancestors were the first to notice fossils

making stone tools would not, at this stage at least, have revealed any petrified remains. There is a continuing debate over whether these first toolmakers were members of our genus *Homo* or more distantly related species of *Australopithecus*. Whoever they were, they were the first geologists and had to know their rocks, learning by trial and error which made the best hammer stones for breaking bones open and which made good choppers for butchering carcasses.

Wherever they moved to, these early stonemasons took toolmaking skills with them. We know that around 2 million years ago the first stone toolmakers to leave Africa were the *Homo erectus* people. By around 1.8 million years ago they had made their way to south-east Asia, and by 1.7 million years ago had extended north into what today is the Republic of Georgia.

Only certain rock types fulfil the essential prerequisites for the basic stone-tool kit of axes, choppers, blades and scrapers: hardness, brittleness and ease of working. Such rocks are not always available everywhere in the world; it all depends on the local geology, something these toolmakers would soon have discovered upon moving into a new region. Whilst many of the ideal rock materials are derived from volcanic rocks, especially a volcanic glass called obsidian, there are some very important and, in certain situations, common alternatives to be found in sedimentary strata.

Chert and flint are the most famous of these and are quite widely distributed through geological strata of all ages from Precambrian, such as the 2.1-billion-year-old Gunflint Chert of Ontario, Canada to Cretaceous-age flints commonly found throughout the chalk rocks of Western Europe. Since these flints and cherts develop in sedimentary strata there is always a chance that they will contain fossils. Their development is complicated, but basically they are glass-like rocks formed from silica-rich gels within seabed sediments. The gels solidify into hard and brittle nodules of various shapes before the rest of the sediment turns into rock, and the nodules often formed around dead organisms, especially sponges and the shells of sea urchins, clams and so on.

If you ever have the opportunity to look closely at broken flint surfaces, perhaps forming a wall or on a flint-strewn beach, there is a good chance that with a sharp 'eye' and a bit of searching you will eventually find some fossils. Our stone toolmaking relatives must have had the same experience whenever they were working flints. As they had to process enormous quantities of this remarkable material, they certainly would have come across fossils. Flint can, with a bit of practice, be flaked to produce blades as sharp as the finest of today's razor blades. The only problem with the flint blade is that a fine sharp edge is very brittle and can only be used once before it needs to be discarded or, if possible, retouched.

Often the presence of a fossil in the rock material made it unsuitable for toolmaking. However, archaeologists have found a number of beautiful flint hand axes, especially in France and England, where the tool has been worked around a fossil to make it an integral but non-functional part of the tool. An excellent example is a 13cm (5in) long flint hand axe found in 1911 at the Norfolk village of West Tofts in East Anglia. The flaking of the nodule to form a bifacial hand axe has been carefully worked around the shell of a small scallop or *Spondylus* clam so that it has a central position in the axe, which is of the Acheulean type and perhaps as much as 200,000 years old.

The process of making such advanced stone tools requires particular cognitive skills such as forward planning and the use of an intermediate stage in manufacture. The concept of what the final tool should look like has to be held in the mind's 'eye' before the end product can be formed.

Sophisticated toolmaking of this kind is cultural rather than inherited and is transmitted from person to person and from generation to generation within a population. Slight variations in technique may creep in and become the hallmark of a particular group.

The careful inclusion of a fossil as part of a tool shows a further symbolic level of concern and interest. Whilst the fossil is a 'found' object, and does not itself require manufacture, the act of integrating it into a made object – the stone tool – is a conscious selection and the final product becomes equivalent to a 'found' work of art. Although normally associated with the advent of 'modern' 20th-century art, it would seem that the technique is perhaps one of the earliest in the development of art.

The conscious manufacture of art objects, along with the manufacture of personal ornaments, the ceremonial burial of the dead and other advanced cultural developments, is normally associated with the first appearance of *Homo sapiens* in Eurasia, around 60,000 years ago. However, it is now known that some of the Neanderthal people made some ornaments and buried their dead with ceremony around the same period. If, as seems likely, the inclusion of fossils in stone tools dates

back as far as 100,000, or, even 200,000, years ago in Europe, then they provide evidence that the Neanderthals had more highly developed cognitive skills than they are often credited with. Recently, consciously manufactured 'artwork' has been found preserved on rock material dating back to 77,000 years ago in South Africa where it was probably made by early modern humans. The 'art' consists of a number of carefully engraved diagonal, criss-crossing lines that form a diamond pattern on a small piece of red ochre. They may just represent a counting device or a symbolic patterning, but they represent another step in artistic development.

Our prehistoric ancestors commonly used seashells as personal ornaments. Many examples have been found in burials associated with early modern humans, members of our species *Homo sapiens*, even dating back as far as 40,000 years ago, and occasionally with some late Neanderthal burials around 35,000 years old. Some of these burial sites are up to several hundred kilometres from

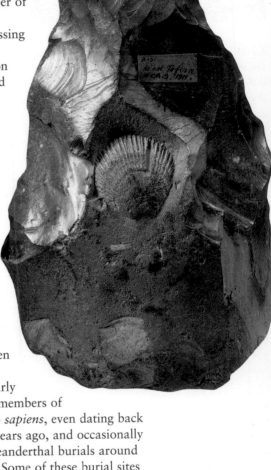

ABOVE:
The monster of Troy with its huge jaws and skull-like appearance, as depicted on an ancient Greek vase

BELOW LEFT:
The oldest known 'artwork', a diamond pattern scratched on a small piece of red ochre by one of our African ancestors 77,000 years ago

BELOW:
Closely resembling the monster of Troy and found on the Greek island of Samos is this Samotherium skull, belonging to a giant Miocene giraffe

the coast. Consequently the presence of seashells would seem to be good evidence of trading between these hunter-gathering peoples, as they are unlikely to have travelled great distances just to collect shells. However, there is a complication here because some of the shells may also be what are technically known as subfossils; that is, they may be many thousands, even several millions, of years old. In many areas of southern Europe well-preserved (subfossil) seashells can be found in old deposits of sands and clays that have not been turned to hard rock strata because they have not been buried, compressed and lithified. Thus it is quite possible that some of the seashells used as personal ornaments were subfossil shells found inland.

We shall never know what our ancestors actually thought such shells were. Perhaps they made a straightforward connection between them and the sort of shells commonly occupied by living snails and clams found both at the seashore and inland. However, by historic times any

such connection was a much more complicated affair. How could seashells occur far from the seashore and elevated high above sea level? What could have brought them to such a position? To make matters worse, the shells were made of material often very different from that of modern shells. We now know that during the process of fossilisation shells may be radically changed in appearance and composition and only retain a superficial resemblance to their original nature.

But there was another more pressing problem associated with the discovery of very different kinds of fossils – large bones found in superficial deposits all around the Mediterranean region of the Classical worlds of ancient Greece and Rome.

Pelop's shoulder blade – fossil giants, real and mythical

The Classical mythology of the Greeks and Romans is full of references to giants, centaurs and other monstrous creatures, all of which have been portrayed in vivid detail in their legends and artwork. Is it all fantasy or might there be substance to some of the stories? We now know that there were many large and some fantastical creatures living in the Mediterranean region during the Ice Age, although most had died out by about 10,000 years ago. Our human ancestors not only saw these creatures but hunted many of them, perhaps to extinction. They are beautifully portrayed in engravings, sculptures and cave paintings dating back as far as 37,000 years ago. Is it possible that Greek and Roman legends were inspired by the discovery of gigantic bones of the so-called Ice Age megafauna, the mammoths and other extinct elephant relatives, the rhinos, big cats and bears which once lived all over Europe and Asia?

When modern humans first appeared in the Aegean region of the Mediterranean around 60,000 years ago, they encountered a rather different geological environment to that which they had been used to in Africa. The geological history of the Mediterranean region is exceedingly complex and is still actively evolving thanks to ocean floor spreading and plate tectonics. The continent of Africa is rotating north-westwards. As a result, the floor of the Mediterranean is being pushed back down into the Earth's interior, generating as it does so the repeated earthquakes and volcanic eruptions that have characterised the region for tens of millions of years.

As a result of this tectonic activity (as geologists call it) some landscapes and parts of the seabed, especially around the Aegean, have been submerged, and others elevated high above sea level to form many of the coastal stratified rocks of the region. Charles Lyell (1797–1875) the 19th-century British geologist, illustrated the Roman pillars at Pozzuoli, near Naples, as a frontispiece for his famous book *Principles of Geology*. The columns would have been bored by marine organisms, showing that they were drowned beneath the waves by earth movements and subsequently elevated again. Many of the Aegean strata were originally deposited in terrestrial or shallow marine environments and are, in places, stacked full of fossil shells and bones, some of which are extremely well preserved. It is quite hard not to notice the abundant fossils in many parts of the Mediterranean.

Until very recently, historians of palaeontology have paid little attention to references made in Classical literature to possible fossil bones, although passing mention is often made as to how the early Greeks understood the meaning of marine fossil shells. However, even recent authors have been puzzled by how the peoples of the Classical world 'somehow... never noticed the huge fossil remains of dinosaurs, mammoths, and other extinct vertebrate species'. The explanation normally provided is that the bones 'were essentially too big to be noticed... or to be taken seriously as bones of animals' (Serjeant in Currie and Padian, 1997).

One story that has often been repeated is the Empedocles myth, in which the Greek philosopher is supposed to have studied fossil elephant skulls from the caves of Sicily. For instance, the American dinosaur specialist Michael Novacek recounts (1996) how 'Empedocles, writing in 400BC, noted that fossil elephant skulls common in the Mediterranean region could be associated

ABOVE:
A French cave painting of an extinct mammoth provides a remarkably accurate 'snapshot' of what they really looked like

LEFT:
Charles Lyell realised that marine mollusc borings in the Serapis temple columns in southern Italy proved that earth movements had severely affected the region

Over 3,000 years ago ancient Egyptians collected fossil bones, wrapped them in linen and placed them in shrines to the gods. This one is now preserved in Bolton City Museum, England

RIGHT:
The central nasal opening in the skull of various elephant relatives has been mistakenly reported as evidence for the Cyclops legend

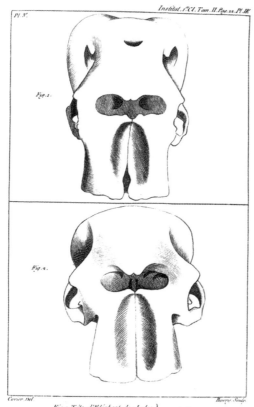

Fig.1 Tête d'Eléphant des Indes } vous de face.
Fig.2 Tête d'Eléphant du Cap }

with the Homeric legend of the Cyclops'. The story is sometimes embellished with the additional claim that Boccaccio was the first to publicise Empedocles's finds.

Curiously, the whole story can be traced back no further than the Austrian palaeontologist Othenio Abel who, in 1914, speculated that the single large nasal opening in elephant skulls might have been for the eye socket of a large one-eyed giant and declared that 'Empedocles reported such finds in Sicilian caves and believed these to be unassailable proof of the existence of an extinct race of giants'. It is possible that Empedocles saw such remains, but there is no record in his surviving writings.

Thanks to an American academic and Classical folklorist, Adrienne Mayor, our ignorance of the Classical record has been corrected. Her recent book – *The First Fossil Hunters: Paleontology in Greek and Roman Times* – has revealed a very different picture. She shows the extent to which fossils were being noticed more than 3,000 years ago.

In the early 1920s the archaeologists Guy Brunton and Sir Flinders Petrie

discovered piles of fossils in Egyptian shrines to the god Seth at Qau and Matmar. Seth was often represented as an anthropoid deity with the head of an unknown mammal. The bones, some of them wrapped in linen, were dark, heavy and polished. They were typical of petrified bones that have been rolled around in river beds. Most were of extinct crocodiles, buffalo, boar and hippos that lived in the area 2 or 3 million years ago. Clearly they had been purposefully collected and given special status by these ancient Egyptian worshippers, although we will probably never know what they really thought they were.

Brunton intended to write a memoir describing the bones, but it never appeared and all record of them seemed to have been lost for good. However, thanks to some clever detective work by Adrienne Mayor, the bones have been found languishing in the stores of the Natural History Museum in London, still packed in their original crates. Hopefully one day they will be properly described as Brunton promised 80 years ago.

Around the same time, during the Bronze Age in Anatolia, the ancient Trojans were sufficiently impressed by fossil bones that they placed one in the citadel of Troy (Hisarlik). In 1870 the German archaeologist Heinrich Schliemann found the fossil when he excavated a burial site in the city, and it has been identified as the backbone of an extinct Miocene whale over 10 million years old. According to Mayor, the find lends weight to Pausanius's story about the magical properties of a relic from

the Greek hero Pelops.

Pausanius (*c.*AD150), a traveller, recounts a story of the Trojan War (*c.*1260BC) in which soothsayers had predicted that Greece would never capture Troy until a relic from Pelops was brought to the city. So the relic, a shoulder blade, was sent for and sure enough victory followed. But on the return journey to Greece the ship was wrecked in a storm and the relic lost. Many years later Damarmenos, a fisherman, hauled up the bone in his net. Amazed by its size, he first buried it in a beach, but eventually went to the oracle at Delphi to try and find out whose bone it was and what he should do with it. By coincidence an ambassador from Elis was there, asking the oracle for a cure

A mammoth shoulder blade looks quite like a human one, and it is not surprising that such bones were mistaken for those of giants

for the plague. The Pythean priestess told him that the Elean people needed to recover Pelops's magical relic and told Damarmenos to hand over the bone. He did so and, as a reward, the Eleans made him and his descendants guardians of Pelops's shrine at Olympia. However, in time Pelops's shoulder blade crumbled away because, according to Pausanius, it had been so long on the sea floor.

Around AD77, the Roman naturalist and historian Pliny the Elder (AD23–79) reported that the shoulder blade was no longer on display at Olympia. As Mayor says, it is highly likely that the bone was from one of the large Ice Age mammals such as the mammoth, *Mammuthus primigenius*, or another extinct elephant that lived in the region. Their shoulder blades can be a metre or so in length and, to the untutored eye, look remarkably similar to human shoulder blades.

From the 7th–5th centuries BC city states all around the Greek world became caught up in a competitive scramble to recover the

remains of their legendary heroes. Chance finds spurred deliberate bone hunting as cities sought to enhance their religious and political status by the peculiar glamour conferred by possession of the remains of their heroes. For instance, the Athenians sought to recover the remains of Theseus from the island of Skyros where, according to legend, he had been murdered. In 476BC the Athenian general Kimon captured the island and searched for the bones. Large bones were found beside a bronze-pointed spear and sword and were duly carted off in Kimon's trireme to Athens. Their arrival was celebrated with processions through the streets to their final interment in the heart of the city.

The Classical literature from Herodotus (*c.*430BC) to Augustine (AD354-430) is full of scattered references to giant bones. Around 200BC Euphorion, a Greek librarian in Antioch who collected legends, told how the Aegean island of Samos was reputed to have been occupied by gigantic and dangerous wild animals called the Neades, 'the mere roar of which could split the ground' and whose 'huge bones are now displayed in Samos'. Much later, around AD100, the Neades legend is referred to by Plutarch, who states that some of the bones are the remains of war elephants used by Dionysus to defeat the Amazons on Samos.

Plutarch's recognition of the bones as those of elephants is by far the oldest accurate identification of such fossils. Mastodon bones do indeed occur in the bone beds of Samos. Euphorion's report was confirmed in 1988 when excavations carried out by German archaeologists uncovered a very large mastodon thigh bone in the ruins of the Temple of Hera.

Thanks to Adrienne Mayor's investigations we can now see that fossils have played a significant role in our developing world view since antiquity, even if it has taken us another 2,000 years and more to recover the evidence. For the peoples of the Classical world, fossils seemed to provide convincing evidence for the veracity of their myths and legends populated by heroes and monstrous beings. But, as we shall see, with the coming of the Judaeo-Christian tradition, fossils were to be given new explanatory power.

Towards the scientific interpretation of fossils

Giant fossil bones found in surface deposits of sands, gravels and clays that we now know belong to the Quaternary Ice Age and somewhat older Tertiary strata below them were still helping to bolster myths, legends and folklore in medieval times throughout Europe. The interpretation had changed slightly as the gods of the Classical world were either not known to the majority of people or were not acceptable within a predominantly Christian culture. Giants such as the Celtic Finn, the Scandinavian Ymir, the Teutonic Hrungnir and the Anglo-Saxon Gog and Magog were still very much part of the ancient and largely pagan folklore. As a result, giant bones were invariably regarded as belonging to the 'local' giant. Sometimes the bones were placed in coffins and reburied in churches or sanctified ground. Others however, were displayed in churches in much the same way as they had been in the pagan temples of the Classical world. Presumably this was part of the church's effort to reduce pagan superstition.

Historical records preserve brief accounts of just some of these finds. For instance, an ancient English chronicler, Ralph of Coggeshall in Essex, recounts how in 1171 the collapse of a river bank revealed bones of such a huge size that he estimated that they belonged to a 'man' who 'must have been fifty feet high'. Similarly an enormous thigh bone, found in 1443 by workmen digging the foundation of St Stephen's cathedral in Vienna, was thought to be that of a giant. The bone was chained to one of the cathedral's doors for many years: it became known as the Giant's Door.

In both instances, the bones were almost certainly mammoth humerus (thigh) bones. Even as late as the 17th century bones and teeth discovered in the south of France (in 1613) were widely exhibited as those of Teutobochus, the giant king of a Germanic tribe defeated by the Romans in 105BC. In 1984, the French palaeontologist Léonard Ginsburg showed that these particular fossils belong to *Deinotherium*, an extinct relative of the elephant.

By comparison with the occasional discovery of such large bones in surface deposits, fossil shells were much more abundant in certain stratified layers of loose sediment and in much older hardened sedimentary strata.

Understandably, there were often considerable problems with interpreting the exact nature of such finds. Although many of the fossils were indubitably similar in appearance to the shells of clams and snails commonly found in present-day marine and freshwaters, there were others that were quite different; and the material substance of many of these fossil shells was different from those of comparable living creatures. Many were clearly petrified – turned to stone – often with crystal growth and no trace of any organic material.

LEFT:
A mammoth thigh bone, inscribed with the motto of Emperor Frederick III and its discovery date, 1443, was placed in St Stephen's cathedral, Vienna, for many years

BELOW:
In 1678 the naturalist Athanasius Kircher thought that humans (the smallest figure, Homo ordinarius) had descended from giants

Gigantis Sceleton
in monte Erice prope Drepanum inventum Boccatio teste 200 cubitorum.

Picturing Pliny the Elder's fossil

Despite the great antiquity of interest in fossils, it was not until around 1557 that the first picture of a fossil or, at least what is generally claimed to be a fossil, was published. This was a woodcut illustration of a cockleshell by Christopher Encelius (Entzelt in the original German), printed in his book *De re metallica* ('on things metallic') by the Frankfurt publisher C. Egenolph. The picture is clearly that of a bivalved clam related to the common cockles of the shallow coastal waters of Europe, ranging from the Baltic to the Mediterranean, species of which belong in the family Cardiidae. The pictured 'fossil' has characteristic strong radiating ribs with intervening narrow gutters, a few well-marked annual growth lines in the older part of the shell, and numerous closely spaced ones on the youngest part. Although only 15 ribs are shown in the picture, the shell is turned slightly so that not all are visible. Since there seem to be around 11 or 12 ribs by the midline of the shell, the total would be between 22 and 24, within the normal range for most cockle species.

The only strange feature of the illustration is the inclusion of a peculiar projection on one side of the hinge line where two clamshells normally join. I think that this feature can easily be explained. Cockleshells, like most other clams, are held together internally by muscles and externally by a tough organic ligament at the posterior end of the hinge. The muscles rot away or are scavenged within a few days or weeks of the animal's death, but the ligament is much tougher and when dried may last indefinitely. Separation of the two valves requires tearing the ligament apart.

I have specimens of cockles that show just such strange projections made of torn bits of dry ligament. The engraving also shows a slight bump projecting at the other end of the hinge, but that is simply the slightly flange-shaped end of the anterior-most rib. What might seem at first glance to be a somewhat crude woodcut is perhaps a much more accurate picture of the right-hand valve of a cockleshell than generally credited.

However, if I am right about the ligament, the implication is that this is not a fossil at all but a 'modern' shell. A projecting piece of ligament, no matter how tough, would not last long enough in a natural beach environment to be fossilised, but could survive in a Renaissance Cabinet of Curiosities such as Encelius may have had access to. Encelius also illustrated a coiled gastropod shell, but this woodcut is somewhat cruder and harder to identify. It is a high-spired form with numerous tight coils. Unfortunately the aperture, which could help identify it, is not illustrated. Without any ornament, it may be the shell of a land snail and, if so, there are also doubts as to whether it is a fossil form.

Interestingly, the shell of a similar living cockle was illustrated by the French naturalist Guillaume Rondelet with a woodcut some three years earlier in his book *Libri de piscibus marinis*. In this work, published by M. Bonhomme in Lyons in 1554, Rondelet described and illustrated a variety of living sea creatures, mostly fish but also some shellfish. The similarity between the two cockle pictures was noted by the well-known Swiss naturalist, Conrad Gesner (1516–65), in his last work *De rarum fossilium lapidum et gemmarum* published in Zurich in 1565. Indeed, Gesner republished Encelius's woodcut – but only to disagree with his attribution.

Encelius's original purpose in illustrating the fossil was merely an attempt to put a 'face' to a much older fossil name, published by Pliny the Elder, but whose text only survives in later copies. Pliny was a remarkable observer of natural phenomena. He died tragically in the eruption of Vesuvius in AD79, overcome by a fast-moving incandescent gas cloud (*nuée ardente*), an event accurately described in detail by his nephew Pliny the Younger. Pliny the Elder's great encyclopaedic work,

Historia Naturalis, dedicated to the emperor Titus, runs to 37 chapters, beginning with cosmology and ending with a list of natural objects, including rocks, minerals and what we recognise as fossils today. There were very few descriptive words to accompany the names and no pictures at all.

Under the name *Chelidonia*, Pliny writes that there are two kinds: *Chelonia* and *Chelonitis*. The former 'is the eye of an Indian tortoise', whilst the latter is 'like a tortoise', and both are claimed to help predict the future and act as a talisman in helping avoid misfortune. *Chelonia* is still used as a generic name for the living and widespread green marine turtle and belongs to a very successful and long-lived group of turtles – the Chelonioidea – that first appear in the fossil record in early Cretaceous times.

Encelius was following the standard Renaissance practice of trying to recover the wisdom of the ancients, and thought that a cockleshell was what Pliny had meant by his *Chelonitis*! As the late Stephen Jay Gould questioned in one of his last essays, the question of how Encelius managed to construe Pliny's description as that of a cockle is something of a mystery, especially as Encelius also notes that the kind of shell he pictures resembles what one of his countrymen refers to as St James's shell, which is a scallop. Anyway, Gesner's great innovation was to make a critical comparison between two illustrations from different books and to conclude that Encelius's illustration 'is the form called *conchae striatae* by Rondelet' and that 'Encelius presents this specimen as a Chelonitis, but not correctly'.

If I am correct about Encelius's cockle being a modern rather than a fossil one, the first person to illustrate a genuine fossil is actually Gesner in 1558. Gesner had planned a much larger work and only intended the short *De rarum fossilium lapidum et gemmarum* to be a preliminary essay. We are lucky to have this work because Gesner was a victim of the plague and died at home in Zurich, leaving a vast amount of unpublished material.

To Gesner and his contemporaries the word 'fossil' (from the Latin 'fossa' meaning ditch and 'fossilis' meaning 'dug up') included any natural object dug out of the ground. That included minerals and what we now think of as fossils: the remains or traces of once-living organisms. Indeed, these early investigators were struggling to make sense of fossil objects that can be very difficult to interpret. The process of fossilisation often obscures the original nature of organic remains and can produce very organic-looking objects that are actually inorganic in origin (witness the recent débâcle over the Martian meteorite 'fossils', now generally regarded as inorganic).

Gesner's Classical training taught him to question and compare the names of different fossils, to try and reduce the proliferation of different names given to the same kind of fossil. This practice of giving all known synonyms has been followed in monographic works on taxonomy ever since. Most importantly, Gesner was concerned with precise identification. He was the first naturalist to systematically illustrate fossils. His problem was that at this early date the normal means of printing illustrations in books was by woodcuts from which it can be difficult to reproduce fine detail. Gesner's stated purpose was that 'students may more easily recognise objects that cannot be very clearly described in words'. Earlier works such as *On the Nature of Fossils* by Georg Bauer (1494–1555, otherwise known as Agricola), published in 1546, just described fossils without illustration and consequently were inadequate for the identification and transmission of such information about the natural world.

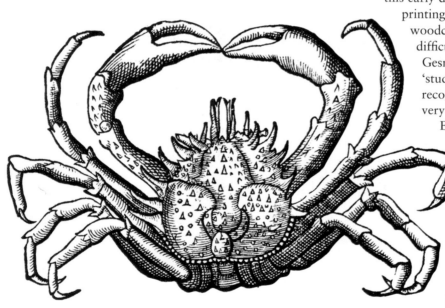

Pagurus la-
pideus, parte
supina expres-
sus.
Ein steininer
Meerkrebß/o=
der Taschen=
krebß.

Gesner had included illustrations of fossil objects in an earlier work, his great four-volume *Historiae Animalium*, published between 1551 and 1558. In 1558, he pictured a fossil crab alongside a living one, and fossil 'tongue-stones' or *glossopetrae* by a picture of a shark (whose teeth they resembled), all of which showed that he was clearly aware of the resemblances. But other similarities were

mistaken according to modern interpretation. Gesner also tried as far as possible to compile his information from first-hand observation or from preserved material, in his case specimens from the collection of Johann Kentmann. Gesner's book is the first to refer to a specific collection of fossils, as he wished 'to encourage other students of these objects... to send me more examples of stones worth recording and suitable for accurate reproduction'. But to Gesner fossils were still very much 'earthly reminders of the jewelled construction of the heavenly city of God'.

Tongue-stones and sharks' teeth

One of the most important early naturalists who helped resolve the nature of fossils was Niels Stensen (1638–86), or Steno, commonly acclaimed as the 'founder' of several of the earth sciences such as stratigraphy, palaeontology and crystallography. He originally left his native Copenhagen in 1660 to study medicine at Leiden in the Netherlands, but like so many peripatetic scholars of the time moved on, to Paris and then Florence, where he took up a hospital post.

Steno's anatomical skills led him to investigate the detailed nature of 'fossils'. With contemporaries such as Robert Hooke, Steno was reacting to the view that fossils were formed by some kind of '*Plastick virtue* inherent in the earth'. Such a view was still actively promoted, for instance in the 1664 popular encyclopaedia on *The Subterranean World* by the prolific and highly successful German Jesuit Athansius Kircher (1602–80). Kircher was also still concerned about trying to calculate how many creatures could feasibly have crammed into Noah's Ark.

Large sharks have been and still are more common in the Mediterranean than most holidaymakers may wish to know. In October 1666 one such beast was landed by fishermen near Livorno. News of the monster reached Steno's employer, the Grand Duke of Tuscany, Ferdinand II, and since the shark had been landed in his 'territory' he ordered its head to be brought to Florence so that it could be dissected by Steno. Without refrigeration the head was not in the best of condition by the time it reached Steno so he could only carry out a fairly cursory examination of its most perishable tissues and organs. But sharks' teeth, like ours, are mineralised and are the only part of a shark that does not readily decay; shark 'bones' are made of cartilage

ABOVE:

In 1675 Athanasius Kircher tried to picture what Noah's ark must have looked like in order to accommodate Noah's family, all the animals and their food

RIGHT:

Steno's 1667 comparison between fossil 'tongue-stones' and the teeth preserved in a dried and somewhat anthropomorphised head of a living shark

which does not fossilise as bone does. Sharks' teeth, known as 'tongue-stones' or *glossopetrae*, are common fossils in Mesozoic and Tertiary strata, especially in some parts of the Mediterranean such as the island of Malta.

As we have seen, Gesner had already made the connection between such fossils and sharks' teeth, but Steno progressed the argument significantly. He showed that there was no evidence that tongue-stones grew in soil or rock; on the contrary, they often showed some signs of decay. Steno demonstrated that the 'earths' in which the fossils were normally found must have been in a soft condition when they first enclosed the tongue-stones. He explained this softness as a result of being mixed with water either at the time of Creation or during the Flood. Consequently he saw no obstacle to the conclusion that tongue-stones were derived from sharks that had died and whose only preservable remains, their teeth, had been caught up in the sedimentation of the deposit. Steno's detailed argument was published in a 1667 treatise on muscles that he had been preparing.

To further the comparison he included an engraving of a shark's head with open mouth showing the rows of teeth in the jaws, along with the virtually identical fossil tongue-stones. Most importantly,

·EIVSDEM LAMIAE DENTES·

Steno presented his argument in a much more modern way than had been previously used for the description of fossils. He listed observable and thus repeatable facts, thereby separating them from speculation. He therefore presented a connected and structured argument leading from observation through inference to conclusion. He said that he was just presenting a case as if in a law suit, and left it open to others to present the opposing case for the formation of tongue-stones within the earth, if they could. In doing this

Steno was clearly aware of questions of method in natural philosophy and was concerned to improve the way such arguments were presented, in much the same way as the mathematicians of the time were also doing.

Steno was also carrying out a detailed study of the rock strata in Tuscany, and was planning a large work on the subject when the king summoned him back to Denmark. He had to make do with the publication of a short *Prodromus (Forerunner)* to his projected *Dissertation on a solid naturally enclosed within a solid*. In this *Prodromus*, published in 1669, Steno stated that 'given an object possessing a certain form, and produced by natural means' his aim was 'to find in the object itself evidence showing the position and manner of its production'. The problem was that what were known as 'fossils' at the time included both organic and inorganic objects.

Steno showed that 'fossils' such as quartz crystals in fact grew by precipitation and crystallisation from saturated solutions in the same way as those produced experimentally in a laboratory. By contrast, 'fossil' shells grew by the 'vital' accretionary and secretionary processes of their animal occupants, and therefore could not have grown *in situ* in the rock.

For the organic origin of fossil shells to be plausible, Steno also had to explain their position inland within rock strata that was high above sea level. From his field studies in Tuscany he argued that strata were originally precipitated on the seafloor as successive horizontal layers of sand, gravel and enclosed shells. This implied that any uplifted and tilted strata found above sea level must be due to subsequent changes, inferring a sequence of events in Earth history.

Steno described two separate periods of horizontal precipitation. The lower, earlier phase, antedated life on Earth and therefore contained no fossils; the later fossiliferous phase was after the creation of life. Each depositional phase was followed by a period of excavation of the underlying strata, and by collapse of the higher and younger layers into the cavity. For the first time fossils and strata were seen as evidence for a history of life.

In his *Prodromus* Steno was also one of the first naturalists to formulate the 'law of superposition', which stated that in any given sequence of sedimentary strata, the bottom layers were laid down first and become progressively younger up through the pile. It was nearly 100 years before this understanding of stratification and their contained fossils was progressed much further – by the English surveyor, William Smith (1769–1839), and his French contemporaries, Georges Cuvier (1769–1832) and Alexandre Brongniart (1770–1847). This law cannot be applied in all environments since the action of plate tectonics and mountain building is able to entirely invert strata on a massive scale. In addition, volcanic igneous rocks may intrude sedimentary strata and other rocks, forming a relatively young layer between two older layers.

However, other problems were being thrown up by new fossil discoveries. Doubts were being raised about those earlier interpretations of large bones, thought to belong to gods or giants. Such fantastical interpretations were no longer tenable in a world of increasing rationality and enlightenment. Natural philosophers such as Newton (1642–1727) were showing that the phenomena of the natural world were no longer inexplicable and intractable problems if tackled with the right kind of methodological approach, such as that employed by Steno.

As we shall see, whilst the emergent scientific method was overcoming some problems of interpretation, gradually revolutionising the prevailing world view and allowing fossils to be seen for what they really are, new difficulties in interpretation arose. Whilst there were explanations of why seashells might be found far inland and even on mountain tops, there were problems of geographical distribution of certain fossil organisms, especially the elephants and their relatives and the big question of extinction. How could a benevolent God allow any of his creatures, which he had designed and created, to become extinct? Part of the problem was that of proving whether extinction had happened or not since there was always the possibility that somewhere, in an unexplored region, survivors might be found.

Fossils can be very confusing. This mould of a leaf-like fossil is just an impression found in 580-million-year-old rocks from Charnwood Forest, England. It may actually represent the remains of a seapen (pennatulacean)

Chapter 2
Extinct monsters

Wandering elephants?

Many of the giant bones discovered in Classical times can now be interpreted as those of extinct relatives of the living elephants, the proboscids, which were much more diverse and numerous in the recent geological past (over the last 40 million years) than at present. Similar finds of large bones made throughout medieval Europe and even as late as the 18th century in North America were still being attributed to giants. However, from as far back as the early 17th century scholars, such as the French anatomist Jean Riolan, were claiming that some of these bones belonged to elephants. The problem with accepting this was the question of how could beasts which, as everybody knew, lived in hot climates, have survived in Europe? One possible explanation was that they were victims of the Flood and had been washed northwards by the floodwaters.

It seemed hard to imagine that elephants might have roamed out of Africa into the 'primeval' forests of Europe but there was increasing evidence that this had happened. In 1630 a huge skeleton was found and excavated at Tunis in North Africa. A French traveller obtained one of the teeth and sent it to a friend, Nicolas Peiresc. Peiresc subsequently recorded how, by chance, a live elephant was being exhibited in France at the time. He noted that its teeth were remarkably similar to the fossil tooth from Tunis. There are a number of additional records of similar finds of giant

bones; some found in Italy in 1687 compared closely with those of a mounted elephant skeleton in a Florentine museum. Evidently elephants had been present in Europe – but there was still the problem of how they got there.

Naturalists searched historical records in an effort to trace their origin, and came across one possible explanation. The Carthaginian general Hannibal had brought elephants to Europe as part of his attack on Rome in 218BC, and the Roman Emperor Claudius also used the big beasts in his invasion of Britain in AD43. Although there was some historic precedent for their occurrence in Europe, the explanations were not particularly satisfactory, especially as the fossil bones were often found buried deep in the ground, suggesting that they were of greater antiquity.

The other most important historical source of elephant-related remains was Siberia from where Chinese merchants had been buying ivory for over 2,000 years. The tribal hunters of Siberia told the Chinese that the tusks belonged to giant rats or mole-like animals that used their tusks to tunnel through the rock-hard frozen ground. The same explanation was still being given to inquisitive foreigners at the end of the 17th century. As we shall see, this apparently fanciful explanation had a basis of truth.

Dutch diplomat Evert Ysbrant Ides, working for the Russian Czar, Peter the Great, was making his way to China in

1692. Passing through Siberia, he asked members of the Yakut, Ostiak and Tungus tribes about the exact origin of the beautiful white ivory that was known to come from the region. The tribespeople spoke of the 'mammut', an animal that lived in tunnels beneath the ground and how '...if this animal comes near the surface of the frozen earth so as to smell or discern the air, he immediately dies. This is the reason that they are found dead on the high banks of the rivers, where they accidentally come out of the ground'.

Ides also recounted how 'mammut' legs and tongues could still be found, especially on the banks of the great rivers, such as the Lena, which drain into the Arctic Ocean. 'In spring when the ice of this river breaks, it is driven in such vast quantities, and with such force by high swollen waters, that it frequently carries very high banks before it, and breaks the tops off hills, which, falling down, reveal these animals whole, or their teeth only, almost frozen to the earth.' Furthermore, the 'teeth' (here referring to the tusks) are 'placed before the mouth as those of the elephants are...'.

Elephants in North America

Even more problematic was the evidence of elephant-like fossil remains in North America, which could not be explained away by Roman history. In 1705 huge bones and teeth were found near New York at Claverack on the banks of the Hudson River. One of the teeth was said to have weighed 2.3kg (5lb), and a thigh bone measured 2.1m (7ft) in length. The Governor of Massachusetts Joseph Dudley alerted the famous scholar and philosopher, Cotton Mather (1663–1728), to the find. Mather wrote an account of the specimens to Dr John Woodward, a well-known London physician and collector of fossils. Woodward (1665–1722) was a Fellow of the Royal Society and summarised Mather's account in the published *Transactions* of the Society, reporting that the tooth 'has four Prongs, or Roots, flat, and something worn on the top: it was six inches high, lacking one eighth, as it stood upright on its Roots and almost thirteen inches in circumference; it weigh'd two pounds four ounces Troy weight'.

In 1765 more giant bones were uncovered at a place called Big Bone Lick in Kentucky. George Croghan, a wealthy Irish trader, whose hobby was collecting fossils, noted in his diary that he had found elephant bones 'in vast quantities... five or six feet underground... and two tusks above six feet long'. He sent some of his specimens to the American diplomat and scientist Benjamin Franklin (1706–90), who was living in London at the time.

RIGHT:
A fanciful 18th-century drawing supposedly of a mammoth, but looking more like an ox with claws and twisted horns, has been attributed to a Swedish soldier who crossed Siberia in 1722

Franklin's interest was aroused, and on 5 August 1767 he wrote to Croghan: 'Many thanks for the box of elephants' tusks and grinders. They are extremely curious on many accounts; no living elephants have been seen in any part of America by any of the Europeans settled there... The tusks agree with those of the African and Asiatic elephant in being nearly of the same form and texture... but the grinders differ, being full of knobs, like the grinders of a carnivorous animal; when those of the elephant, who eats only vegetables, are almost smooth. But then we know of no other animal with tusks like an elephant, to whom such grinders might belong.'

These were acute observations and Franklin went on to point out the different geographical and climatic distribution of living elephants compared with the fossil forms. He explained the discrepancies 'as if the earth had anciently been in another position, and the climates differently placed from what they are at present'. Franklin had picked up an important distinction in the teeth of the North American fossil elephants. They were indeed different from those of both living elephants and the Eurasian mammoths.

Croghan had also sent specimens to an English scientist, Peter Collinson, who lectured on the problem of their identity to the Royal Society in London on 10 December 1767. Collinson adhered to the more traditional explanation that the peculiar distribution of the fossil elephants in the cold regions of North America, Europe and Asia was due to the torrential currents of the Noachian Deluge which had swept them north from their normal habitats. He was more adventurous in his conclusion that the unusual features of the North American teeth showed that they 'belong to another species of elephant, not yet known'.

As we have seen, right up until the mid-19th century the catastrophic action of the Deluge, as described in the Old Testament, was the generally accepted explanation for the occurrence of fossilised remains of life being trapped in rock strata. And there was another problem: how could a benevolent God allow any of his creations to fail and become extinct? In the 18th century, with

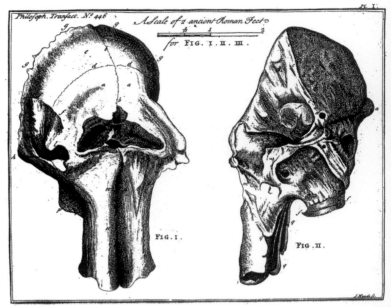

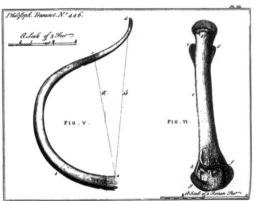

ABOVE & LEFT: *Accurate early illustrations of mammoth bones (skull, tusk and thigh bone) were made by the German naturalist Daniel Messerschmidt and published in the 1741 Philosophical Transactions of the Royal Society of London. The pictures prompted Cuvier's 1799 comparison between living elephants and mammoth*

so much land and ocean still unexplored, there was still the possibility of apparently extinct creatures lurking somewhere in the far reaches of the Earth.

Another eminent American, Thomas Jefferson (1743–1826) – like Franklin, a man of many parts – was greatly interested in the problem of the fossil elephants. He also distinguished between elephants and mammoths but did not realise that the 'knobbly' teeth of the North American fossil elephant belonged to yet another kind of elephant-related animal. Jefferson thought that the American fossils belonged to the same kind of elephant as the Siberian fossils, namely the mammoth. He also thought it possible that living mammoths would be found in the unexplored forests and mountains of the great North American continent. When he was president, Jefferson instructed Meriwether Lewis and William Clark to search for live mammoths whilst on their famous expedition to the interior

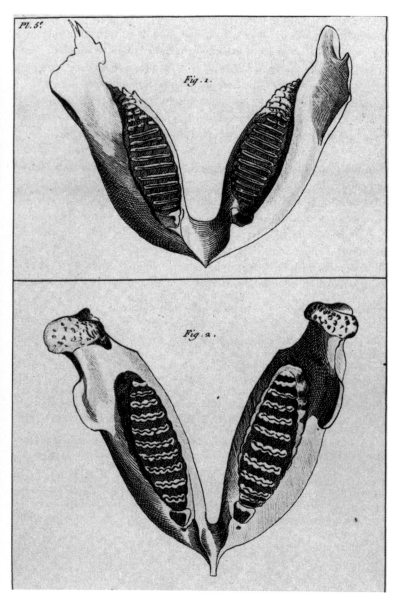

Pl. 5.

Fig. 1.

Fig. 2.

ABOVE:
Cuvier's 1799 comparison between the jawbone of a mammoth (top) and an Indian elephant (below), showing significant differences

Johann Friedrich Blumenbach (1752–1840), of the University of Göttingen, had made a particular study of the fossil elephants of Europe. In 1799 Blumenbach noted that the European bones were certainly those of an elephant but were sufficiently different to those of the African and Asian elephant to warrant being named as a new species *Elephas primigenius*, meaning 'the first born of the elephants'.

At the same time Georges Cuvier was considering the problem of extinction and the identity of these fossil elephants. Cuvier subscribed to the catastrophic flood story as an explanation for the occurrence of the variety of fossil animals he found buried in sedimentary rock strata around Paris. But he also realised that there must have been more than one flood to distribute the fossils at various levels within the rock strata.

Cuvier paid particular attention to the form of the jaws and cheek teeth of the elephant. By comparing jaw form and patterns of ridges on the tooth grinding surfaces he showed that the African and Indian elephants were sufficiently different to be separated by both genus and species, namely *Loxodonta africana* and *Elephas maximus* respectively. Then he showed that the fossil elephants were in turn different enough from either of the living species to be a separate and extinct species, for which he accepted Blumenbach's name of *Elephas primigenius*. Cuvier went on to distinguish the North American fossil elephant with 'knobbly' teeth as a separate genus that he called *Mastodon*, meaning 'breast-shaped tooth'.

from 1804 to 1806. Jefferson insisted that 'in the present interior of our continent there is surely space enough' for such huge creatures. Unfortunately he was wrong; the last of North American mammoth-related beasts had died out some 12,000 years before. The last of them were not hidden away in the deep forests of the high interior but stranded on offshore California Channel Islands, where they lived from 30,000 to 12,000 years ago and became dwarfed in the process because of the shortage of food.

Naming the beast

Meanwhile one of Germany's greatest 18th-century naturalists and experts on fossils,

Siberian elephants

At the end of the 18th century the chief of the Siberian Tungus people was a man called Ossip Shumakov. An important source of income for the tribespeople was fossil ivory, often so well preserved that it was as good as ivory from living elephants. For hundreds of years ivory was traded with passing merchants; it is likely that most of the ivory that circulated in medieval Europe and Central Asia came from Siberian sources. The tribespeople scoured the banks of the rivers that flowed during summer through the permanently frozen terrain of Siberia bordering the

Arctic Ocean. Every now and again bones, tusks and occasionally bodies appeared as the permafrost soils melted. The deeply superstitious tribespeople associated these bodies with bad luck, but the lure of the ivory tusks tended to overcome any hesitation about approaching the cadavers in order to remove the tusks. They may also have spread the bad-luck stories to try and discourage anyone else from removing the elephants' tusks.

In 1799 Shumakov found just such a body embedded in the icy banks of the Lena River whilst he was searching for mammoth tusks. He returned to the spot in 1803 to find the remains of a huge mammoth lying on the river bank. He told a local ivory dealer, Roman Boltunov, and together they removed the tusks the following year. Boltunov was so impressed by the beast that he made a rough sketch of its appearance. Two years later a Russian scientist, Mikhail Ivanovich Adams, who was passing through Yakutsk, heard about the mammoth and sought out Boltunov who showed him the drawing.

Adams was equally impressed and realised that such a find could help make his name back in St Petersburg, so he set out to recover as much as he could of the beast. Unfortunately by the time he got back to the site the cadaver had attracted

other scavengers. Wolves and foxes had eaten most of the flesh, and some had been cut off by Yakut hunters and fed to their dogs. Luckily the skull was intact and retained some skin, one eye and an ear. More skin and flesh lay beneath the animal and Adams managed to remove it along with 16.8kg (37lb) of reddish, woolly under hair and long, black, coarse outer hair. The skeleton was intact apart from the beautifully preserved tusks and these he managed to buy from Boltunov. They are over 3m (10ft) long. Everything was dispatched back to the St Petersburg Academy of Sciences, where Adams taught botany.

In 1808 the skeleton of this magnificent bull mammoth was reassembled in the Academy's museum of zoology, along with skin from around the eye and ear. The Adams mammoth, as it became known, was the first mammoth skeleton to be mounted and put on display. It still stands there, nearly 200 years later, over 5m (15ft) long and over 3m (10ft) high. The magnificent creature was about 45 years old when it died, maybe 30,000 or more years ago.

The discovery of the Adams mammoth explained the presence of elephant relatives so far north. With their thick woolly coats they were well adapted to the cold (as the French naturalist Buffon had previously

LEFT:
Adam's mammoth as drawn by Roman Boltunov in 1804, suggesting that originally much of the flesh remained

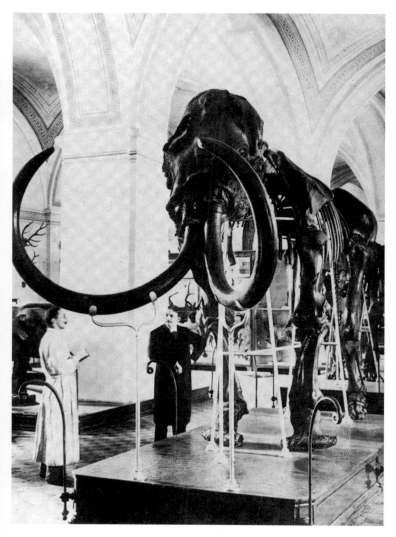

Mammoths were between 2.75–3.4m (9–11ft) high, weighed 4 to 6 tons and generally looked rather like the living elephants. There were some important differences but only a few of these showed up in the skeletal remains. Their forelegs were longer than their hind legs so that the back sloped down towards the rear. It would have been difficult to ride on the back of a mammoth, whereas living elephants have much more horizontal backbones.

Mammoth tusks were often spectacularly long and curved. A tusk recovered from the Kolyma River in Siberia measures 4.2m (14ft) along the curve from tip to root and weighs 84kg (185lb). By comparison the largest African elephant tusks rarely reach more than 3m (10ft) in length or weigh more than 60kg (27lb). Female mammoths, like female elephants, were generally smaller than the males and have smaller and lighter tusks.

The most obvious differences between elephants and mammoths were only realised fully when soft tissue was recovered from the frozen mammoth corpses of Siberia and Alaska. Most striking of mammoth characteristics was their long hairy coat that consisted of a coarse outer layer of hair up to 1m (3ft) long in places. Below was a thick and shorter woolly underlayer, about 2.5–8cm (1–3in) long. The overall appearance of the coat would have been like that of the living musk ox, which is now restricted to Arctic Canada. Living elephants are born with a covering of hair over most of the body but they soon lose most of it.

Mammoth hair is clearly an adaptation for body insulation and is accompanied by several other features that helped protect the animals from the cold. Below the skin lay a thick fat layer 8–10cm (3–4in) thick which is not seen in elephants but is similar to that found in marine cold-water mammals. The mammoth had small ears, which were only about 38cm (15in) long, about 15 times smaller than that of the African elephant. The tail is also shorter with between 7 and 12 fewer vertebrae. Also, mammoths had a distinct fatty hump on top of their shoulders and a curious topknot of fat and long hair right on top of the skull. One other external distinction

suspected). But Cuvier raised the question of why, if they were so well adapted, had they become extinct? His explanation was that the ancient world had suffered repeated catastrophic revolutions. Just as the *ancien régime* had been swept away in France by the progressive forces of the Revolution, so such fossil remains proved to Cuvier 'the existence of a world anterior to ours, destroyed by some kind of catastrophe'. For Cuvier that catastrophe was either a sudden inundation by the sea or a sudden drop in temperature, which would explain why the mammoth bodies were often found in frozen ground.

Mammoth characteristics and statistics

Strangely, despite the association of the name with enormous size, the mammoth was no bigger than an African elephant.

WATERHOUSE HAWKINS, Del.

POST-TERTIARY DEPOSIT. 1. MAMMOTH, ELEPHAS PRIMIGENIUS. 2. HYÆNA SPELÆA. 3. HIPPOPOTAMUS MAJOR. 4. URSUS SPELÆUS. 5. MACHAIRODUS LATIDENS.

was the tip of the trunk which in mammoths has two long prehensile, finger-like, projections which were used for fairly delicate manipulation or selection of plant material for eating. By comparison, the living elephants have only one short projection at the end of the trunk and tend to curl the whole end of the trunk when plucking plant food.

When the first cave paintings and engravings of the animals of the Ice Age 'game park' were discovered in the 19th century, especially in south-west France and northern Spain, mammoths were amongst the most common beasts to be portrayed. All the distinctive features of the mammoth body were accurately depicted by the Cro-Magnon, early modern humans, who clearly knew the beasts intimately. Human hunting activities may well have contributed to the untimely demise of most of these wonderful beasts by 10,000 years ago.

The very last of the mammoths

Although most of the mammoths had become extinct, they were not all gone. In 1989 a Russian geologist, Sergei Vartanyan, explored the extremely inhospitable islands of the Arctic Ocean, 200km (125 miles) north of Siberia and well inside the Arctic Circle, looking for well-preserved mammoth bones that would be good for radiocarbon dating. On Wrangel Island he found tusks, teeth and leg bones lying partly embedded in the permanently frozen tundra soils (permafrost). He noticed that some of the bones looked strangely small for mammoths but was even more surprised when he dated the bones. Their radiocarbon ages ranged from 7,380 to 3,730 years old, long after the mammoths were supposed to be extinct. Vartanyan showed the remains to a colleague, the Russian palaeontologist and mammoth

ABOVE:
Waterhouse Hawkins's illustration of some of the extinct animals of the Quaternary which he hoped to model life size for the Crystal Palace display in Sydenham, south London

One of the earliest pieces of prehistoric artwork to be found, an engraving of a mammoth on a piece of ivory from the famous Cro-Magnon site of La Madeleine, France, and illustrated by Edouard Lartet in the 1860s

expert Andrei V. Sher.

A comparison of the size of some of the teeth and estimates of the age of the animals they belonged to suggested that even when quite old they stood no more than about 1.8m (6ft) high, compared with a typical height of 3–3.4m (10ft–11ft) for an adult mammoth. When the Russians published their results in 1993, they claimed that a population of mammoths had crossed onto Wrangel when the sea level was lowered during a glacial phase of the Ice Age.

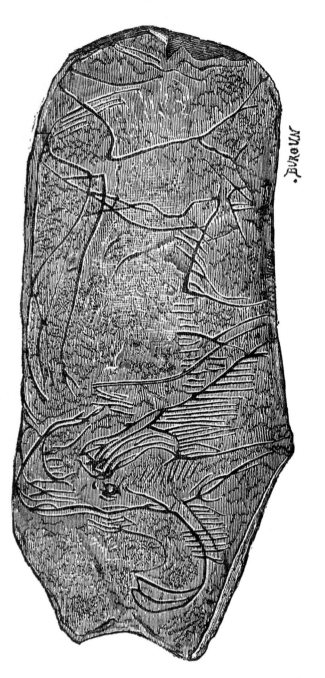

Subsequent rising sea levels stranded the animals on the island and over many generations dwindled and they eventually became dwarfed. This phenomenon has been described in several other island situations, with extinct giant deer becoming similarly dwarfed on the Channel Islands, off the French coast, after the Ice Age, and elephants and hippos becoming dwarfed on some of the Mediterranean islands such as Malta and Sicily.

It is extraordinary to think that whilst the pyramids were being constructed in Egypt, mammoths were still living on Wrangel Island. The very remoteness of the island had protected them from humans but in the end they too died out. Whether they ran out of food resources or whether they were eventually killed off by humans is not known. President Jefferson was only a few thousand years out in his search for the mammoth.

The last few years have seen a number of attempts to recover good-quality mammoth DNA from frozen cadavers in the hope of cloning them, using living elephants as surrogate mothers. Despite a great deal of hype, no tissue worth speaking of has been recovered. Furthermore many experts feel that the whole project is misguided and that it is much more important to try and conserve the few remaining large mammals that we have, rather than try and manufacture a chimaera, which never would be a mammoth, even if the very complex process of cloning were to work. Cloning of living sheep and other animals has already shown that the whole process is fraught with problems.

The Beast of Maastricht – Napoleonic war booty

The first and by far the most famous sea monster ever to be found was a huge fossil skull dug out of a chalk mine at Maastricht in the Netherlands in 1780. The massive skull, subsequently called the 'Grand Beast of Maastricht', has 1.6m (5ft) long jaws armed with an impressive array of wickedly curved teeth, serrated like steak knives. By the end of the 18th century this prototype 'Jaws' had become so well

known that it was seized by Napoleon's armed forces and carried off to Paris as war booty. The original specimen can still be seen in the National Museum of Natural History in the rue Buffon, Paris, one of the greatest science museums of the world. The Dutch have to make do with a plaster cast.

The importance of this fossil find was immense. The jaws were so big and so different from any others known at the time that they quickly became the focus of arguments about extinction. Today the question of extinction is no longer contentious; practically every seven-year-old knows about the extinction of the dinosaurs. But in the 18th century it was a real problem: how could a benevolent God allow one of his own creations to fail and disappear?

Problematic fossil remains had been found before but most of them were relatively small; and there was always the possibility that they were the remains of creatures that still existed somewhere on the Earth. Neither the depths of the oceans nor the hidden 'depths' of the world's vast forests had been fully explored at the time. On the other hand, most of the giant sea creatures (sharks and whales), and large land animals (elephants, giraffes and so on) were fairly well known by the end of the 18th century, even to people in Europe. Since nothing like the Maastricht monster

was known, there was a distinct possibility that it was no longer alive, even if it was one of God's creations.

But there was another good reason why the 'Beast' attracted so much attention – what kind of animal was it?

Finding the Beast

The fossil jawbones were found deep within the chalk rock of St Pieter's Mountain, overlooking Maastricht. The low chalk hills around the town have been extensively mined and quarried for centuries, the soft white limestone being easy to dig out. By leaving natural pillars and walls, extensive passages and chambers with self-supporting roofs have been excavated. The many kilometres of passages within the hills have been used for all kinds of storage, even concealing people in times of danger.

The skull was found at the same locality in 1780, 30m (almost 100ft) below ground and some 150m (over 490ft) from the entrance to one of the mines. A German military surgeon, Dr C. K. Hoffman, heard rumours of its discovery and paid the miners to recover the block of rock containing the skull.

The news quickly spread and came to the attention of a local clergyman, Canon Godin, who owned the land above the mine. Godin claimed that the specimen was

ABOVE:
A dramatised reconstruction of the 1780 discovery of the first 'Jaws', those of a gigantic extinct marine reptile from underground chalk workings near Maastricht in the Netherlands

even further afield to the New World.

In 1795 Napoleon's invading Republican armies drove off the Austrian army that was defending Maastricht and lay siege to the town. Such was the fame of the 'Grand Beast' that the French General Pichegru ordered his gunners to spare the château, its chapel and famous fossil. Pichegru's concern for the safety of the 'Beast' was not entirely altruistic. He knew that 'securing' it for the 'greater glory of the Republic' would go down well in Paris.

Meanwhile Godin, fearful of the notorious acquisitiveness of the French forces, had hidden the specimen elsewhere. Not to be outdone, the canny Pichegru put up a reward of some 600 bottles of wine (no doubt looted war booty) for the specimen. The 'Beast' duly turned up. Once safely in his hands, Pichegru spared no time or effort in making sure that the Beast of Maastricht was safely transported to Paris. Naturally the French scholars, including Georges Cuvier, were delighted.

Identifying the Beast

Straightaway naturalists recognised that the skull had a very puzzling mixture of features. It was not even clear whether the 'Beast' was a mammal or a reptile. A Dutch

ABOVE:
One of the goals of the Naploeonic forces besieging Maastricht in 1795 was the capture of the fossil jaws of the 'Grand Bête'. They succeeded, and the jaws have been in Paris ever since

BELOW:
The slightly displaced and broken lower jaw (1m/3ft in length) of the Maastricht fossil, showing the conical pointed teeth of a predator

rightfully his and, when Hoffman refused to hand it over, took him to court. Godin's insistence on his moral right to the fossil won him the support of fellow clergymen. Hoffman lost the case and the fossil and had to pay costs.

Godin built a chapel in the grounds of his château to house the skull and enable interested visitors to view it. Over the next few years the 'Grand Beast' was an object of curiosity and 'pilgrimage' for the scholars of the day. It soon became the scientific sensation of the decade. Despite frequent wars there was nonetheless considerable international communication at that time between scholars throughout Europe and

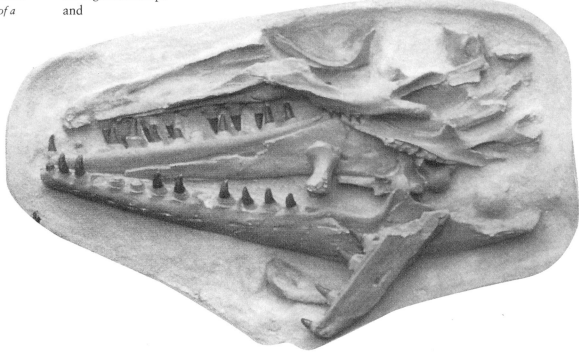

naturalist and anatomist, Pieter Camper (1722–89), had been first to publish an analysis of the fossil in the 1786 *Transactions* of the Royal Society in England. He pointed out characters that significantly differed from those found in living crocodiles and concluded that the 'Beast' was a whale. His diagnosis started a long-running academic argument, especially with French scholars, who thought that it was a crocodile.

In 1799 Faujas de Saint-Fond (1742–1819), one of the French scholars who had welcomed the 'Beast' to Paris, did describe it as a crocodile. But only a year later Camper's son Adriaan claimed (from a more detailed study of its bone structure) that it was actually neither a mammalian whale nor a reptilian crocodile but another kind of reptile: a lizard. This was a revolutionary conclusion, since although some living lizards were known to be capable of swimming, there were no known

lizards anywhere near this size or so fully adapted to life in the sea.

Camper based his conclusions on the newly emerging science of comparative anatomy. Since the realisation that all backboned animals had similar basic skeletal plans, it was possible to compare how particular bones, such as arm bones, can be adapted for different modes of life in different animals (for example for swimming in seals, flying in bats and walking in dogs). Camper wrote to Georges Cuvier, telling him of his conclusions.

Cuvier had agreed with Saint-Fond's diagnosis of the 'Beast' as a crocodile and he rejected Adriaan Camper's startling suggestion – to begin with. But evidently he felt obliged to re-examine the evidence, and when he did so was forced, albeit reluctantly, to agree with the younger Camper. This is one of the very few instances when Cuvier changed his mind in the lights of another naturalist's work.

TOP:

The Maastricht fossil reconstructed as a crocodile by Faujas de Saint-Fond, a diagnosis disputed by the Dutch naturalist Adriaan Camper

ABOVE:

Another reconstruction of the Maastricht animal, this time as a lizard-like reptile; although nearer the truth; it was actually a marine (not a landliving) animal, up to 17m (56ft) long

Cuvier attempted to cover up his volte-face by bluster and he scornfully dismissed the earlier diagnosis of both Saint-Fond and Camper's father. By naming the 'Beast' *Mosasaurus* in 1808, meaning 'lizard from the River Meuse', Cuvier made sure that 'his' interpretation would persist. He went further in his diagnosis than Camper and suggested that *Mosasaurus* was a monitor lizard lying somewhere between the iguanas and varanids. Cuvier also used the mosasaur to illustrate his conviction that extinction had occurred.

By the 1840s mosasaur fossils were found in Britain and North America, and by 1874 the first record from New Zealand showed that these particular sea monsters had spread worldwide and been extraordinarily successful top carnivores.

Understanding mosasaurs today

The mosasaurs were the most impressive and largest of the predatory marine reptiles, growing to over 17m (56ft) in length with jaws of up to 1.9m (6ft). Not all were predators; some species have been found with almost hemispherical teeth, an adaptation for crushing the shells of clams and other shellfish picked off the seabed.

Comparison of bone structure has shown that different mosasaurs occupied different levels within the oceans and seas of the late Cretaceous. *Clidastes* and *Tylosaurus* were deep-water fast-pursuit predators, whilst *Platecarpus* was a shallow-water ambush-hunter and lay in wait on the seabed for passing prey.

There is independent fossil evidence for the general savagery of these top carnivores. Tooth marks, on the fossilised shell of the giant turtle *Allopleuron hoffmani*, and healed jawbone fractures in a number of mosasaur specimens, suggest that they were fairly indiscriminate predators. They seemed to have engaged in potentially lethal male-to-male combat probably over access to females. The fact that some of them survived jaw fracture shows that they must have had rapid recuperation rates, like crocodiles today.

For such a successful group, the mosasaurs' existence was very brief: some 27 million years. They were just at the point of an enormous radiation when they disappeared abruptly at the very end of the Cretaceous, 65 million years ago. Like the dinosaurs, they were replaced quite quickly in Tertiary times by marine mammals.

Whilst the mosasaur discovery was of considerable historical importance, it was also something of a lucky 'one-off' find as mosasaur fossils, especially complete skeletons, are relatively rare. Of more lasting significance was the discovery at the beginning of the 19th century of fossils belonging to some different groups of marine reptiles. These new fossil forms were much more complete than the early mosasaur finds and they rekindled both scientific and public interest in the exotic nature of these ancient monsters of the deep sea.

Sea dragons – 'denizens of the abysmal slime'

Long before dinosaurs were 'invented' by the British anatomist Richard Owen (1804–92) in 1842, the idea that extinction had occurred in the past was given a considerable boost by the discovery of fossil skeletons of strange marine reptiles in the Jurassic strata of England that we now know to be over 180 million years old. These spectacular fossil 'sea dragons' were amongst the first extinct life forms to stir public imagination and be of real intellectual concern. Portrayed as 'denizens of the abysmal slime', the image of these monsters of the deep became icons for the 'gothic' imagery of the first popularisers of palaeontology. It is perhaps no accident that several monsters beloved by cryptozoologists today, such as Scotland's 'Nessie', bear an uncanny resemblance to early 19th-century images of sea dragons.

Late 18th-century Northern Europe provided a suitable intellectual and cultural climate to promote public interest in the idea of the remote geological past and its inhabitants. It was largely a result of the nature of the geology of the Low Countries of France, Germany, Holland and England that determined the initial direction these discoveries should take. The exposed and most readily available fossiliferous rocks of these areas are of Jurassic or younger age.

The limestones, sandstones and shales of the coastal cliffs and inland hills have been

ABOVE:
*John Martin's
wonderfully 'over the
top' Gothic
reconstruction of extinct
marine reptiles for
Thomas Hawkins's
1840 Book of the Great
Sea Dragons*

quarried for millennia. Stone fortifications and other 'public works' were built by the Romans and Normans along with the churches, cathedrals and castles of medieval Europe. The late 18th century saw a renewed demand for rock as a raw material not just for fine buildings but for more general construction related to Britain's growing wealth. Apart from dimension stone, which was so expensive that it was mainly used just for the façades of significant buildings, bricks were increasingly being used. In addition, increasing shortages of suitable timber for traditional timber-framed construction promoted the manufacture of bricks from clay. Large-scale brick manufacture not only requires large volumes of suitable clay but also a more efficient fuel than wood. The whole growth of the industry was part and parcel of the Industrial Revolution and the exploitation of coal as a fuel. Many new quarries were excavated and landowners came to realise the value of a whole range of geological materials lying beneath their green fields. Inevitably this quarrying and mining activity greatly

enhanced the chances of finding important new kinds of fossils, and – most importantly – there was a growing interest in these finds.

Since the European Secondary (now known as Mesozoic and Tertiary) strata that were being quarried are largely marine sediments, most of the fossil finds were of creatures that lived in ancient seas. If the Mesozoic strata had been made of terrestrial deposits full of dinosaurs (as in much of the Midwest of North America) the history of discovery would have been very different. As it was, the dinosaurs had to 'wait their turn'.

First recognition of the Jurassic System dated back to observations made by the pioneer German explorer and geographer Alexander von Humboldt (1769–1859). At the end of the 18th century, as he travelled around the flanks of the Alps, through south-eastern France, western Switzerland and northern Italy, Humboldt noticed that the limestones of the Jura mountains seemed to form a distinct rock unit in their own right, which he called the *Jura-Kalkstein*. However, it was not until 1839 that there was a more widespread use of the name Jurassic on the continent with the publication of a general description of 'Jura' strata in Germany by another German, the geologist Leopold von Buch (1774–1852).

The British outcrop of Oolitic limestones and Liassic shales, belonging within what is recognised today as the Jurassic System of strata, stretch from the north Yorkshire coast at Whitby, southwards through the Lincolnshire Wolds, then south-westwards across the country where they form the picturesque rural landscapes of the Cotswolds, then south to the Dorset coast. Strange crocodile-like petrifications were reported from coastal strata at both ends of the outcrop by the 17th-century naturalist John Ray (1627–1705). The Oxford scholar and Keeper of the Ashmolean Museum, Edward Lhwyd (1660–1709), illustrated marine reptile vertebrae in his 1699 book *Lithophylacii Britannici Ichnographia*. The fossils probably came from strata exposed along the banks of the River Severn which we now know were deposited at the end of Triassic and the beginning of Jurassic times. Lhwyd thought they were fish backbones and so he called them *Ichthyospondyli*.

There are a number of other historical records of isolated fossil bones and even parts of skeletons being found during quarrying operations throughout much of

the English outcrop and in Germany during the 18th century and occasionally they were pictured in books. Often this is the only reason we know anything about them because few of the actual specimens have survived or can now be identified in existing museum collections. An extensive collection was made by the famous Scottish anatomist John Hunter (1728–93) and was bought by the British government in 1799 for £15,000. It formed the Hunterian Museum of the Royal College of Surgeons in London, and the catalogue compiled by Richard Owen in 1854 shows that it contained 29 specimens of marine reptile fossils. Unfortunately most of the collection was bombed into oblivion in 1941, during World War II.

By the beginning of the 19th century, whilst such finds were regarded as the remains of marine creatures ('the irresistible proofs of an Universal Deluge, and of a new world risen from the ancient ocean...'), it was not clear exactly what kind of animal they belonged to: they could be crocodile, lizard or even whale. The problem was soon to be resolved.

Constant erosion of coastal cliffs in Yorkshire and Dorset, especially by winter storms, broke fossils from their rock tombs and tumbled them onto the beaches. Those which were not quickly recovered were soon pounded to unrecognisable pieces by

RIGHT:
The limestone and shale strata in which the Annings found their fossils exposed in the cliffs near Lyme Regis in southern England

the waves. Local people, who traditionally scoured the beaches for anything useful or saleable, were well aware of these strange shells and bits of bone. However, it was not until the latter part of the 18th century, when fossils acquired some value, that the locals bothered to recover the heavy and awkward petrifications from the beaches. Some of the most spectacular of these early discoveries came from Lyme Regis at the southern end of the outcrop, where many of them were found by a remarkable Dorset family, the Annings.

The Anning family

Between 1811 and 1830 the Anning family found and recovered several strange, vaguely dolphin-like skeletons from the Liassic limestones and shales that form the local sea cliffs of this part of southern England. Richard Anning (1766–1810), the father of the family, was a carpenter and cabinetmaker by trade but was often out of work. His wife Mary (called Molly by the family) tried to supplement their precarious income by collecting and selling fossils to the growing numbers of genteel tourists. In

the late 18th century, changing agricultural practices and enclosures of land meant that many of the peasants of rural England were impoverished.

People such as the writer Jane Austen (1775–1817) and her social circle increasingly frequented picturesque fishing villages like Lyme, to admire the seascapes, the quaint cottages and their inhabitants whose local accents were barely understandable. It was becoming fashionable to collect natural curiosities to adorn glass cabinets in the reception rooms of spacious homes. The specimens could always be brought out as aids to polite conversation. Typical of their time were the three Philpot sisters who first visited Lyme in 1806 and became avid samplers and collectors of natural objects. Somehow, the Philpot ladies met Mary's daughter, also confusingly called Mary, and befriended her. Over the following years they bought numerous specimens from young Mary and her family. Eventually the Philpot sisters' magnificent collection of fossils was donated to Oxford University Museum.

But there were other collectors who took a more serious financial or academic interest in the more unusual specimens. One of these collectors, James Johnston, wrote in 1810 to a friend that 'there is a person at Lyme who collects for sale by the name of Anning, a cabinetmaker and I believe as men are, may be depended upon, I would advise you calling upon him...' By comparison, he also remarked that nearby at Charmouth there was 'a confounded rogue of the name of Lock to call upon... give him a Grog or a Pint, this will buy him to your interest and all the crocodiles he may meet with will almost assuredly be offered to you first, you must then agree with him for he is poor and will sell within one hour after the article is found'.

The Annings probably had as many as 10 children but such was infant mortality for poor families in those days that only two survived to maturity: Joseph (1796–1849), who became an upholsterer, and Mary (1799-1847). Disaster struck the family again late in 1810 when Richard died from the combined effects of consumption (tuberculosis), then a common disease, and a serious fall. He left his family in serious debt to the tune of £120, with the result that they were dependent on parish relief until 1816. Nevertheless, in 1811 Joseph found the spectacular skull of a fossil 'sea dragon' and the following year his sister Mary, just 12 years old, found the rest of the skeleton. According to a report in a local newspaper, workmen employed by the family dug it out of the rock in November 1812.

The specimen was sold for £23 to the lord of the local manor, Henry Henley, who was a keen fossil collector. He sold it on to William Bullock, a showman, who exhibited the petrified curiosity in his private London Museum of Natural History. Natural history was fashionable and people were prepared to pay to go and see the newly discovered wonders of the natural world. The fossil was illustrated and described by Sir Everard Home, brother-in-law of John Hunter, in 1814. Home noticed some crocodile-like features in the jaw but concluded that its affinities lay with the fish. When Bullock's collection was sold to the British Museum in 1819, the specimen was priced at £47 5/-, a great deal of money in those days. The specimen now has pride of place in the Natural History Museum in London.

More and better finds of 'saurians' were made; one particularly fine ichthyosaur was sold in 1819 for £100 and the Annings' fame spread amongst scholars and collectors. Mary probably had little or no schooling and yet, of necessity, she had learned to read and write and was able to communicate news of finds to those who might be interested. Lyme was still very much off the beaten track and a long way from London by horseback or carriage. Most of her clients were well-educated gentlemen and her surviving letters are testimony to her abilities that went far beyond finding specimens; she corresponded and conversed over matters of scientific detail.

The most spectacular and interesting specimens went to 'Oxbridge' academics such as Adam Sedgwick (1785–1873) and William Buckland (1784–1856), who used them to develop their ideas about life in the geological past. It is a matter of record that many

RIGHT:
A lithograph from 1825 showing a young woman, thought to be Mary Anning junior, 'fossicking' on the beach with a hammer

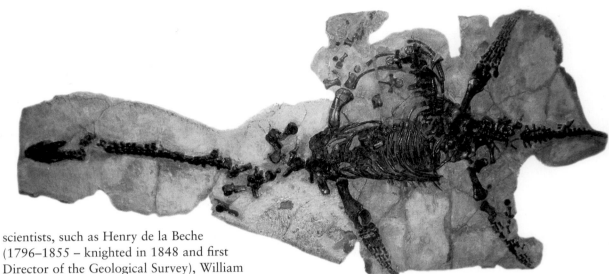

scientists, such as Henry de la Beche (1796–1855 – knighted in 1848 and first Director of the Geological Survey), William Buckland (first professor of geology in Oxford), Louis Agassiz (1807–73 – a famous Swiss geologist, particularly interested in fossil fish) and even the King of Saxony, visited Mary's small shop to see her latest specimens and talk of fossils. Many of them remarked upon her knowledge of anatomy, especially of the marine reptiles, and she was not afraid to dispute the finer details of interpretation even with the likes of Professor Buckland.

One of her best finds was a complete 3m (10ft) long plesiosaur in 1823. Henry de la Beche and the Reverend William Conybeare (1787–1857) had previously realised that certain bones, thought to belong to an ichthyosaur, were in fact those of a quite different reptile. They called this putative creature *Plesiosaurus* (Greek for 'near lizard') but its recognition was disputed by other scholars. De la Beche and Conybeare were greatly pleased when Mary proved them right in their suspicions by finding this complete specimen.

The following year Conybeare described their new fossil and concluded correctly that it was a marine reptile that swam slowly, using its flippers, a bit like a turtle. He considered that its long flexible neck compensated for its small head and weak jaws by being able to bend quickly and snap up passing prey. He also took the stance of many churchmen of the time who were enthused by natural science. In these pre-Darwinian days, Conybeare regarded the extreme deviation of the plesiosaur body from the reptilian norm as a perfect and purposeful example of design by the Creator. It exemplified the 'exquisite orderliness and diversity of divine creation'. Conybeare and his fellow clergymen could pursue their interests with a clear conscience in the knowledge that they were investigating and illustrating the works of God for the greater edification of mankind.

Mary Anning's social status and sex prevented her from entering this developing world of 19th-century science that was rapidly becoming professional and was dominated by university-educated, middle-class men. Mary never married and there is much speculation of a tragic romance with a gentleman (subject of Sheila Cole's 1993 novel *The Dragon in the Cliff* and John Fowles's *The French Lieutenant's Woman* in 1969) but no real evidence. She found at least three complete ichthyosaurs (1818, 1821 and 1830); two plesiosaurs (1823 and 1830); a cephalopod *Belemnosepia*, with its fossilised ink sac preserved; the first British

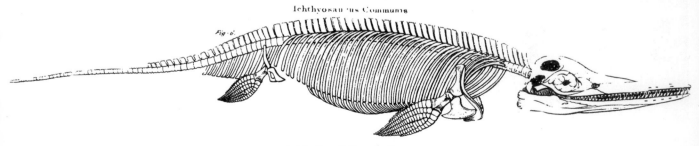

Ichthyosaurus Communis

Fig. 6

pterodactyl *Dimorphodon* (1828); the cartilagineous fossil fish *Squaloraja* (1828) and quantities of other invertebrate shells. Mary Anning was possibly the first person to recognise the phosphatised fossil fish and reptile faeces that are not uncommon in the Lias shales. How much of her observation found its way, unacknowledged, into the scientific books and papers that Buckland and others wrote, is a matter of argument; but she certainly felt that her knowledge had been used.

Until recently very few of her fossil finds, specimens of which are in museums, have been recognised. It is only now, when museum curators are more interested in the history and provenance of their specimens, that her discoveries are being properly acknowledged. Of the five most important institutions to purchase her finds, only Oxford University Museum has a direct record of a specimen originating from her, and that is a single coprolite. Over the last few years searches of Mary's correspondence have revealed that Cambridge University's Sedgwick Museum has several

of her prize ichthyosaur specimens.

Her latter years were a sad time; there was a general decline in interest in fossils and she made no further spectacular finds, so her income fell. She suffered from breast cancer and had to give up the hard life of 'fossicking' on the beach. Fortunately her gentlemen had not entirely forgotten how much they owed to her. She became a worthy cause, and at the meeting of the British Association for the Advancement of Science in 1835, £200 was raised by private subscription. Buckland persuaded the Prime Minister Lord Melbourne to add £300 in 1838, and together these sums bought an annuity of £25. She died in 1847 at the age of 48. The most famous lines that may refer to her are those of the well-known tongue-twister:

She sells seashells on the seashore
The shells she sells are seashells,
*   I'm sure*
For if she sells seashells on the
*   seashore*
Then I'm sure she sells seashore shells.

BELOW:
An 1843 reconstruction of a Jurassic seascape crammed with fossil lifeforms, ranging from flying pterodactyls to sealilies and other shells on the seabed. The land is populated with turtles, crocodiles and plants such as cycads and horsetails

Chapter 3

Humans before Adam

Homo diluvii testis – *fossil evidence for the Flood*

As we have seen, the only possible human-related fossil bones found by the beginning of the 18th century had been recognised as belonging to other non-human animals, especially fossil relatives of the elephants. However, the apparent lack of human fossils was something of a puzzle. According to the generally accepted world view of the Judaeo-Christian tradition, the history of Creation and the subsequent Flood were clearly described and accepted as an historic truth. All the human sinners and other lifeforms that were not saved by being taken into the ark were drowned. If this provided an historic explanation for the nature and existence of fossils, the fossil remains should include those of the human sinners – so why were they not found?

For most of the three millennia and more of the Judaeo-Christian era, priests have told Bible stories to illiterate congregations. From mediaeval times, Christian churches provided some illustrations for the stories through various media such as sculpture, stained glass and illuminated manuscripts, but the latter were only seen by a very select few. Not until the growth in literacy and the development of cheaper means of reproduction was it possible for a wider readership to have personal access to the texts and illustrations.

One of the finest early examples of an illustrated account of the Creation story

Johann Jacob Scheuchzer, the famous Swiss naturalist, portrayed in his 1730 book Physica Sacra *with specimens as evidence for the Creation*

BELOW:
Thomas Burnet's 1684 view of the Earth during the Flood, with Noah's ark just stranding on Mount Ararat

was published by the Swiss naturalist Johann Jacob Scheuchzer (1672–1733). He trained as a physician in Zurich and made one of the largest collections of fossils in early 18th-century Europe. Scheuchzer travelled widely in the Alps and wrote extensively on the natural history of Switzerland. Like most of the naturalists of the day, he firmly believed that fossils were the relics of the Deluge and provided evidence for the historical reality of that event. His 1709 book *Herbarium of the Deluge* depicted a wide range of fossil plants that he thought were victims of the Flood.

Puzzled by the lack of human fossils from the Deluge, Scheuchzer seized upon the discovery of a

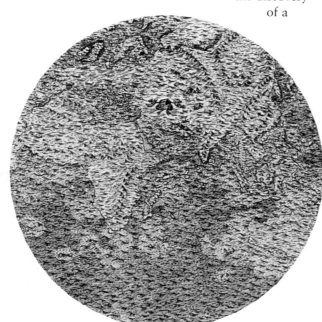

1.2m (4ft) long human-like fossil in strata being quarried for lithographic stone at Oeningen by Lake Constance. In 1725 he described and illustrated the fossil skeleton as *Homo diluvii testis* – meaning 'A Man, a Witness of the Deluge and divine Messenger'. To Scheuchzer the skeleton was the 'rarest relic of the accursed race that must have been swallowed up by the waters'. It seemed to show a flattened skull, backbone and parts of the limbs, all crushed within the fine-grained muddy limestone strata. It was the first fossilised remnant of a putative human relative to have been found.

From 1731–3 Scheuchzer published his last and largest work *Sacred Physics* in Latin, German and French, which became widely known throughout the literate world. The biblical narrative is illustrated with 750 full-page copper engravings, the majority of which depict history as it is told in the 1611 'Authorised' version of the Bible from the Creation through to the Apocalypse. Since this was before the renaissance in scholarly biblical criticism, Scheuchzer's was a largely literal reading of the story, providing a detailed pictorial sequence from initial chaos to a complete human world.

Genesis 1, verses 1–31, in the Old Testament describes the sequence of events. Day one saw the creation of darkness and light, day two the heaven and the waters. On day three dry land was formed and called 'earth', and through the

RIGHT:
According to Scheuchzer this fossil, found in 1725, is 'the bony skeleton of one of those infamous men (Homo diluvii testis) whose sins brought upon the world the dire misfortunes of the Deluge'

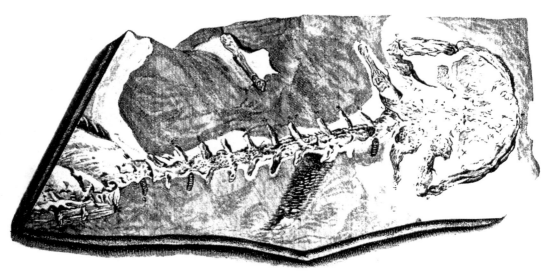

'gathering of the waters' seas were made. Then God said (verse 11), 'Let the earth produce fresh growth, let there be on the earth plants bearing seed, fruit-trees bearing fruit each with seed according to its kind'.

Scheuchzer describes the scene: 'In this Third Day, we see the surface of the Earth raised up, the waters running down from the slopes of the hills... but the Earth is still quite naked and uniform, with none of the ornament of a painting, and with its dirty colour even inspiring a certain horror. However, this silt was a rich nursery; this muddy water was at the same time pregnant and nourishing; the Earth was fertile, so that plants of all kinds could grow there; and in a moment it took on an attractive verdure, enamelling the Earth with colours: but nevertheless without having itself the power to produce everything'.

Scheuchzer's is a typical early 18th-century view in which rocky unproductive mountains are abhorrent and beauty resides in lush productive lowlands. To emphasise

the significance of God's gift of seed-bearing plants, Scheuchzer frames his picture with graphic details of the sequence of wheat germination from embryo to seed head ready to harvest.

Day four saw the creation of sunlight for day and starlight for night. On the following day five God said (verse 20), 'Let the waters teem with countless living creatures, and let birds fly above earth across the vault of heaven'. He then created '...the great sea-monsters and all living creatures that move and swarm in the waters, according to their kind, and every kind of bird'. Here Scheuchzer is at pains to point out that fish '...were not in any way produced by the power of the water itself. The only thing that the waters contributed was the place; the structure is the work of God'. Two pictures show fish, whales and flying fish, and separately a variety of shellfish, displaying the variety of nature as revealed by naturalists of the time.

On the final day six of his creativity, God said (verse 24), 'Let the earth bring forth

ABOVE LEFT:
Scheuchzer produced the first illustrated account of the Creation in his 1730 book Physica Sacra. *Accordingly, the third day saw the formation of dry land and the gathering of the waters to form seas*

ABOVE RIGHT:
Day three continued with the creation of very European-looking flowering plants, apart from the odd palm. The fossil record does not preserve flowering plants until late Jurassic times

ABOVE LEFT:
On day five the fishes (including mammalian whales) and birds were created, and Scheuchzer frames the picture with the fishes you would see in any well-stocked Mediterranean fish market

ABOVE RIGHT:
Day five also saw the creation of shellfish with accurate drawings of living clams and snails taken from a collection rather than from live observation

living creatures, according to their kind: cattle, reptiles, and wild animals, all according to their kind'. Then God said, 'Let us make man in our image and likeness to rule the fish in the sea, the birds of heaven, the cattle and all wild animals on earth, and all the reptiles that crawl upon the earth... be fruitful and increase, fill the earth and subdue it, rule over the fish in the sea, the birds of heaven, and every living thing that moves upon the earth. I give you all plants that bear seed: they shall be yours for food. All green plants I give for food to the wild animals, to all the birds of heaven, and to all reptiles on earth, every living creature'.

Scheuchzer comments that, 'The work of the sixth day birds, fishes and insects have more similarity to Man than plant; quadrupeds, and reptiles of the serpent kind, approach still closer to Man than fish and birds. Thus we ascend by degrees from the structure of plants and animals to that of Man. The most noble of all creatures, the Microcosm or epitome of all this great

World, now makes his appearance in the Theatre of the World: now that the table is fully spread, the host can be seated...' Firstly he pictures an exotic Edenic or Arcadian scene in which wild animals – including lion, bear, leopard, crocodile and snake – pose with none of 'nature red in tooth and claw' but rather in a Rousseau-like peace and harmony, lacking only the human presence.

Secondly, a lush and very European scene is presented with nothing fiercer than horses, a beaver, rabbit and birds, plus a naked Adam. The frame has a detailed anatomical series of the development of the human from embryo to child. The quality of the illustrations is very high and consequently the whole presentation of the Creation story is very sophisticated with its elaborately detailed natural history. Here early science is acting clearly as the 'servant' of the creator to bring his work to a wider audience, and it worked. Scheuchzer's book became very widely read, especially in its French version.

The Deluge – before and after

The other most important Bible story that impacted upon the interpretation of rocks and fossils is that of the Deluge and ensuing Flood. Genesis recounts the story of Noah and how 'man had done much evil on earth' so that God decided that, 'This race of men whom I have created, I will wipe them off the face of the earth – man and beast, reptiles and birds. I am sorry that I ever made them'. But Noah had won the Lord's favour (Genesis 6, verses 5–9, verse 16), and God said (6 verse 17), 'I intend to bring the waters of the flood over the earth to destroy every human being under heaven that has the spirit of life; everything on earth shall perish. But with you I will make a covenant, and you shall go into the ark... and you shall bring living creatures of every living kind to keep them alive with you.' (7 verse 11) 'All the springs of the great abyss broke through, the windows of the sky were opened, and rain fell on the earth for 40 days and 40 nights.' (8 verse 17) 'The flood continued upon the earth for 40 days, and the waters swelled and lifted up the ark so that it rose high above the ground... more and more the waters increased over

the earth until they had covered all the high mountains everywhere under heaven... every living creature that moves on earth perished, birds, cattle, wild animals, all reptiles and all mankind. Everything died that had the breath of life in its nostrils; the waters began to subside. The springs of the abyss were stopped up, and so were the windows of the sky; the downpour from the skies was checked.'

Firstly Scheuchzer depicted the ark, with its specifed size of three storeys, already sealed up as the rains began to fall and the remaining people who had not been taken on board bewailed their fate. In 1709 he illustrated the scene when the waters began to subside.

Mountaintops have appeared above the waters and there are trees growing on them. In the foreground a dove holds a twig of laurel in its beak. According to Genesis the dove returned to Noah (who had earlier released her) with the 'newly plucked olive leaf in her beak. Then Noah knew for certain that the water on earth had subsided...' Noah and his family left the ark (9 verse 1) and God said to them, 'Be fruitful and increase, and fill the earth. The fear and dread of you shall fall upon all wild animals on earth, on

ABOVE RIGHT:
Finally, we see the creation of mankind with dominion over all other life. Scheuchzer included an anatomically accurate drawing of a foetal skeleton, apparently weeping

ABOVE LEFT:
The final (sixth) day of creativity began with cattle reptiles and wild animals and was portrayed rather as a southern European scene with a few exotic animals such as the lion, leopard and bear

incomparably more ancient, more important and more reliable than those of all the coins of Greece and Rome'.

The emotional appeal and drama of the Flood story still had the power to capture the imagination of people in the early decades of the 19th century. Artists such as the English painter John Martin (1789–1854) and poets such as Lord Byron (1788–1824) were able to exploit this explosion of romanticism. Martin in particular, thanks to the technical innovations of mezzotint engraving, was able to turn the dramatic images of his vast canvases into affordable prints for the wider and growing middle classes who could not easily see the original paintings in London. Themes such as *The Fall of Babylon* (1819), the destruction of Pompeii by the eruption of Vesuvius in AD79 (1822) and the *Deluge* (1826) and its mezzotint version (1828) were hugely successful. Martin even provided an explanatory booklet to go with the print of the *Deluge*, which shows no sign of any doubts about the veracity of the story. He was not interested in literal truths; this was high romantic drama.

As a pictorial genre it continued well past its literal 'sell-by' date with the work of artists such as Gustave Doré (1832–83) who were still illustrating Bibles with such scenes in mid to late century. However, other people were having doubts about the biblical texts; and the veracity of Scheuchzer's famous 'witness of the Flood' was in doubt as well.

Cuvier could tell from Scheuchzer's illustration that the fossil was not human and published a report in 1809, identifying the fossil as that of a giant salamander. After Scheuchzer's death his collection was sold to Teyler's Museum in Haarlem, which Cuvier visited in 1811. Being something of a showman, Cuvier took the opportunity to demonstrate the predictive power of comparative anatomy to debunk *Homo diluvii testis* in front of an audience. He told his audience that if as he claimed the fossil was that of a salamander, the genus *Proteus*, rather than a human, it should have a very distinctive shoulder girdle and pelvis. As Cuvier later wrote, the director of the museum Mr van Marum 'allowed me to uncover the parts hidden in the stone'

ABOVE:

The story of Noah's ark was very much part of the Judaeo–Christian world view that was accepted as an historical truth by most naturalists until the early decades of the 19th century

all birds of heaven, on everything that moves upon the ground and all fish in the sea; they are given into your hands'.

Scheuchzer commented that, 'among the innumerable relics of the Deluge that we now collect and carefully preserve, one finds many that clearly prove that the Deluge began in Spring, and more precisely in May. I have published elsewhere many of my own collection; here I show some more...' The frame of his first Deluge picture illustrates some fossils of plants and insects. The foreground of the second post-Flood picture shows shells and fishes washed up on the rocky foreshore of a mountaintop. As Scheuchzer points out, such fossils stranded high on mountainsides far from the present-day sea coasts, 'are new kinds of coins, the dates of which are

which revealed that the fossil was undoubtedly that of a 'giant aquatic salamander of an unknown species'.

Doubts grow

Any reading of the Old Testament account as a literal or historical truth does have its problems that were recognized long ago. The creation of light before the creation of the Sun (Genesis, verse 1, lines 3 and 16) worried scholars in the 5th century, and the fact that the moon is not light emitting but light reflecting was acknowledged by Calvin in the 16th century. By the latter part of the 18th century scholars, especially in Germany, turned their critical attention to the biblical texts. They found different components to the Genesis account: for example, Genesis 1 combines eight creative actions into six days of Creation, requiring two acts of Creation on two days, the third and the sixth. Furthermore, there are two versions of Creation, one in which God created by uttering commands and another in which he operated as a craftsman. Many other internal inconsistencies and problems with translations and interpretation began to appear so that the literal value of the

texts as historical documents began to be questioned.

Instead the Creation story gradually came to be seen as a myth in the sense that it is not so much an intellectual truth but a truth that allowed believers to cope with living in difficult social circumstances and an often dangerous world. Faced with storms, floods, droughts, heat, disease and death, the inhabitants of the ancient world tried to domesticate the world of nature. This was done partly by naming things, classifying them and telling stories that set mankind within a meaningful cosmic framework; but a framework within which the order of things is entirely subordinate to one God.

One of the biggest challenges to the authority of the biblical account of the Flood came in the latter part of the 19th century when, in 1872, George Smith of the British Museum in London lectured on *The Chaldean Account of the Deluge* from a Babylonian text known as the *Enuma Elish*. Dating from around 3,600 years ago, this ancient text recounts a flood event with very similar details to that of the Noachian deluge but predates it by around a thousand years, since the Genesis story is

BELOW:
*Upright apes – in 1616
the Italian philosopher
Lucilio Vanini was
burned at the stake in
Toulouse for the
heretical suggestion that
humans originated from
apes*

BELOW RIGHT:
*Linnaeus was the first
naturalist to attempt to
arrange all known life
forms into a
classificatory scheme
which has subsequently
been adopted as the
basis for animal and
plant taxonomy*

historically constrained to about
2,900–2,400 years ago. Now it turns out
that the biblical account of the Flood is
only one of numerous flood stories, most of
which are older than Genesis.

Carl Linnaeus – sapient man – puts life in order

The scientific name for humans is *Homo
sapiens*, meaning 'wise or knowledgeable
man', and was 'donated' to us in 1758 by
the Swedish naturalist Carl Linnaeus
(1707–78) when he extended his new
classificatory system of nature beyond the
mineral and vegetable kingdoms to include
that of the animals. In a moment of
supreme confidence and with a degree of
arrogance, he offered himself, a white
northern European male, as the exemplar
for the whole of humanity. Whether there
was a slight hint of irony in Linnaeus's
choice of name is doubtful, but he provided
a wonderfully succinct description for our
species that was more of a prescription
since he simply said, 'Know thyself'. We are
still struggling to do so.

Although Linnaeus was a devout
Christian, for him humans were still
animals and, in the terms of anatomical
classification, barely distinguishable from
apes. Accordingly in God's ordered world it
should be possible to fit humans into some
category within a hierarchical scheme of
classes, orders, genera and species.
Inevitably there were protests from some
more orthodox naturalists. Only 140 years
earlier, in 1616, the Italian philosopher
Lucilio Vanini (1584–1619) was declared a
heretic and burned at the stake in Toulouse
for professing that humans originated from
apes. In the more enlightened cultural and
religious climate of northern Europe
Linnaeus felt intellectually strong enough to
challenge his critics to find any fundamental
differences between chimps and humans.
We now know that we share some 98% of
our genetic make-up with the chimps,
implying (according to the molecular clock)
that we share a common ancestor who lived
some 6 million years ago in Africa.

For over 240 years Linnaean pigeon-holing of living organisms and the use of the Latin binomial with the genus name (for example *Homo*) first, followed by the species name (such as *sapiens*) with heirarchical clustering has been the common language of biology. How else can biologists around the world be sure that they are talking about the same thing if they cannot give each kind of organism, living and fossil, a unique name associated with a formal description and illustration of what it looks like? There was much confusion until Linnaeus first formalised the system in 1735.

For Linnaeus, as for many naturalists working in the cultural and religious climate of Protestant northern Europe, it was a moral duty to investigate and interpret the 'munificent' works of the Creator. For 18th-century naturalists there was no question that the Creator would be anything other than benevolent and rational. Accordingly all his creations, the Earth and its inhabitants, must have been formed according to some meaningful order. It was up to 'sapient man' to discover this natural world and its underlying order.

All organisms that can interbreed to produce fertile young belong to the same species. Linnaeus believed in the fixity of species. He did not invent this way of naming plants and animals but he was the first to attempt its systematic application to all known organisms. To begin with, as a botanist, he confined his effort to plants.

In Linnaeus's time the taxonomic world of known plants seemed sufficiently mappable for him to attempt to include every living one in a single volume. His book *Systema Naturae* was first published in 1735. Because new creatures were constantly being discovered, many of them by Linnaeus himself, he had to produce new expanded editions of his great book. The work gradually gained him an international reputation and he was appointed professor of medicine and botany at the University of Uppsala in 1741.

In 1744 Linnaeus tried to explain how the world came to be stocked with all its plants and animals. Not finding the ark story very convincing, he conflated the Creation and the Flood stories, imagining that all life originated on a mountainous tropical island, surrounded by a primeval ocean. The height of the mountain produced a sequence of climates, becoming more severe with increasing altitude and accommodating a range of life from tropical forms (such as palms and monkeys) at the base to polar ones (such as reindeer

BELOW:
In 1758 Linnaeus included humans, apes and fanciful beings all together in the Order Anthropomorpha. He was not able to critically assess false travellers' reports, just as we still have stories of yetis and 'big feet'

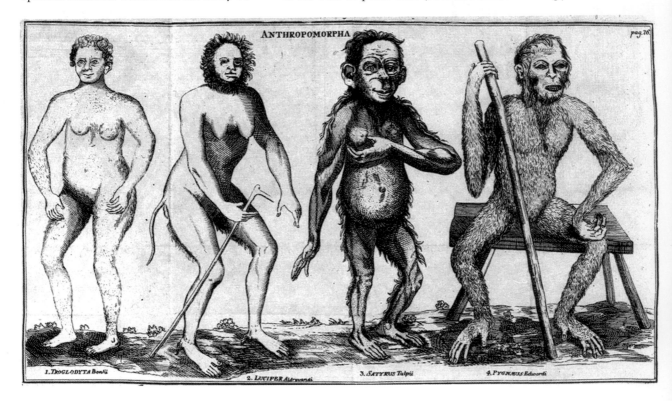

ANTHROPOMORPHA

1. *TROGLODYTA Bontii*   2. *LUCIFER Aldrovandi*   3. *SATYRUS Tulpii*   4. *PYGMÆUS Edwardi*

*The 1698 illustration
and description of
chimp anatomy by
London physician
Edward Tyson
accurately pointed out
48 common features
between chimps and
humans*

and lichens) at the top. Thus the mountain was a miniature version of the Earth as a whole, and when the 'Flood' waters subsided the survivors spread out to repopulate the globe. Although such climatic zoning of life from tropical to polar was discovered in the early 1800s by Alexander von Humboldt and Aimeé Bonpland (1773–1858) in Peru, the rest of the story soon fell apart.

For Linnaeus and most naturalists of the time, species as fixed entities were each created and designed by the deity for a particular purpose and place within the grand scheme of things, ascending from the lowest to the highest. (No prizes for guessing where humans stood on the ladder!) Sometimes organisms were found which did not fit easily into any of the existing categories and so new ones were made and named for them. Consequently the whole hierarchical scheme was constantly getting bigger and more crowded, with new categories especially at the lower taxonomic levels. A single volume was no longer big enough to contain them all and no one naturalist could hope to keep track of everything. By 1758 the *System of Nature* had gone through 10 editions. Even so, as far as Linnaeus could tell, life still consisted of not many more than 4,200 species of animals and 7,700 species of plants.

Not until he reached that 10th edition, published in 1758, did Linnaeus extend his classification to animals and mankind. *Homo sapiens* was grouped along with another human species *Homo troglodytes* and the chimpanzee, which Linnaeus called *Satyrus tulpii* in the order Anthropomorpha. *Homo troglodytes* was a kind of taxonomic 'shaggy dog', a fanciful creature based on rumour and exaggerated travellers' reports. The chimpanzee had been known and scientifically described in the West since 1698, when a young and sickly chimp was shipped to London. The poor beast died and a London physician, Edward Tyson (1650–1708), dissected its corpse and provided the first accurate description of the chimp anatomy and skeleton. Tyson also demonstrated and listed 48 features that chimps have in common with humans, compared to 27 for monkeys and humans.

To Linnaeus this remarkable degree of similarity between the chimp and human fully justified his association of the two in the same order of Anthropomorpha (later changed to Primates, where they still are classified). Today we know that *Homo sapiens* is the one surviving species within the genus *Homo*, which, at present, includes some five or six other extinct species such as *Homo neanderthalensis* and *Homo erectus*. Our genus is in turn one of

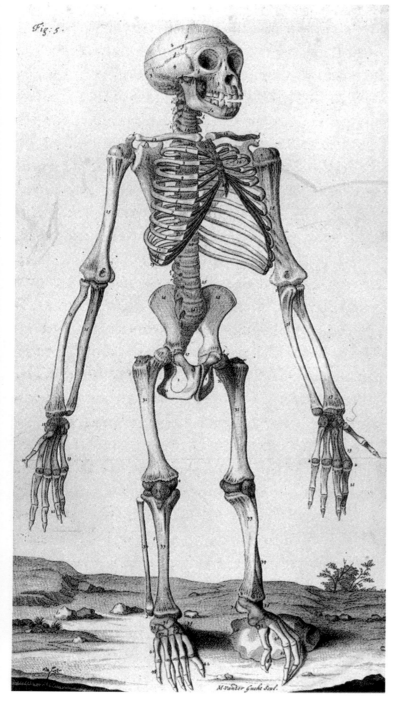

Fig: 5.

M vander Gucht Sculp.

many (other living genera include *Gorilla*, *Pongo*, *Pan* and the extinct *Australopithecus* and so on) in the superfamily Hominoidea, which along with the monkeys and lemurs and the like belongs in the order Primates and the class Mammalia.

Primates

The name 'primate' is derived from the Latin *primatus*, meaning 'of the first rank' or 'chief', which is why Linnaeus, being as hominocentric as the rest of us, used the word, which we also use for the head of a church.

Understanding the biogical characteristics that distinguish humans from the rest of the mammals is not a great problem. However, the zoological group of Primates is more diverse than most people realise, especially when the extinct fossil forms are taken into account. Most of us in the West only experience our nearest biological relatives, the monkeys and apes, in zoos or on film, and so our knowledge and understanding is very limited. There are no living primates native to North America, northern Eurasia or Australasia today, although 47% of fossil primates come from North America and Europe. I suspect that this geographical fact has subtly influenced our Western ideas and attitudes towards our relatives. The Japanese, by comparison, have a much closer relationship and understanding of primates and have been seriously studying them for much longer. This is partly due to familiarity, since the macaques are native to the Japanese islands, and is partly religious, in that the Japanese have fewer ideological problems with accepting monkeys and apes as 'other' rather than 'lesser' beings as the Judaeo-Christian tradition sees them.

The Primates are an order of mammals and equivalent to the bats (chiropterans), rats (rodents) or hedgehogs and their relatives (insectivores) from which they evolved well over 50 million years ago.

Within the Primates there are now 13 families, 64 genera and some 256 species. Our living relatives include not only the familiar apes, monkeys and lemurs, but also the less familiar tarsiers, lorises and galagos, as well as a number of important extinct

groups such as the tarsier-like omomyids and the more lemur-like adapiformes. The problem today is how all these groups relate to one another and whether we can see any clear evolutionary picture.

A new statistical analysis of the fossil record supports the idea of the last common ancestor of the Primates having arisen some 81.5 million years ago in late Cretaceous times, which is close to the divergence estimated from the molecular clock. The analysis (Simon Tavaré et al, *Nature* 2002, 416, pp726–9) also suggests that no more than 7% of all primate species that have ever existed are known as fossils. This is partly due to lower preservation rates of mammals in the Cretaceous compared to Cenozoic times, but is also related to the general difficulty of preserving small terrestrial vertebrates in the rock record, especially those that live in tropical environments. This bias probably has considerable significance for our understanding of the early evolution of groups such as the Primates. At present the fossil record of early Primate evolution comes mainly from North America and Europe whose Mesozoic and Cenozoic rock

ABOVE:
The French anatomist and natural historian Georges Cuvier's contribution was particularly important in linking the study of living and fossil animals and illustrating them accurately

BELOW:

The rock slab with Scheuchzer's human 'witness to the flood' before Cuvier prepared it

BELOW RIGHT:

In 1809 Cuvier 'dissected' Scheuchzer's specimen and revealed that it is in fact the skeleton of a giant salamander

records are the best known in the world. The picture has emerged in which Primates evolved during Palaeocene times in northern continents (which then enjoyed a subtropical climate) and then migrated southwards. But if this picture is heavily biased by preservation, it is possible if not probable that Primates originated much earlier in southern tropical regions, which have a very poor fossil record. They would only have migrated northwards when the climate allowed.

The missing victims of the Flood

One of Georges Cuvier's certainties was that evolution had not taken place since he could find no evidence of any gradual modifications between organisms. Another was that the rise of 'Man' and civilisation was a recent event which post-dated life's other revolutions and the extinction of whole tranches of past life. There were no human remains to be found amongst the debris of the Flood, the flotsam and jetsam of animal shells and bones, the leaves and woody tissues of plants that make up the fossil record. Cuvier had debunked the main contender for a fossilised human, Scheuchzer's *Homo diluvii testis*, in 1809 when he demonstrated that it was no more than the skeleton of a giant salamander.

Within the context of Revolutionary France, with its polarisation between those

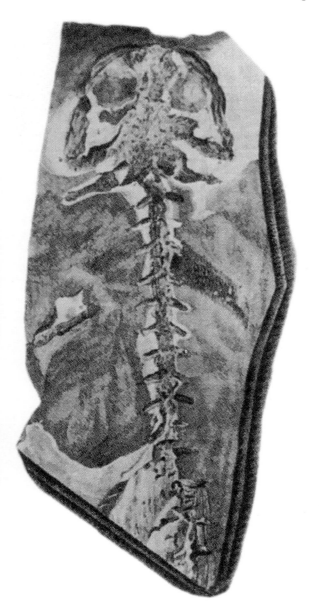

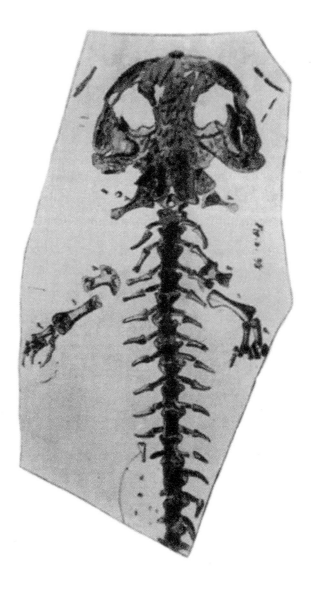

who rejected religion and those who retained the dominant Catholic faith, Cuvier was unusual in being a Protestant believer. He was also very much a product of the time and made a clear separation between faith and science. In this he was unlike so many of the British scientists at the beginning of the 19th century who still were endeavouring to reconcile their geological discoveries with the Old Testament accounts. Cuvier was aware of the new 'science' of biblical criticism that was being developed in Germany and was further undermining the historicity of the biblical accounts.

Fossil evidence for pre-Diluvial humans was slowly revealed during the first decades of the 19th century. However, decades were to pass before they were accepted for what they were, even by the scientific community of the day, because of the overwhelming belief in the Judaeo-Christian tradition and the idea that humanity was fundamentally different from all the other animals and had been specially created.

A Suffolk handaxe

However, Cuvier was unaware that a literally 'ground-breaking' find had been made at Hoxne in East Anglia that debunked his claims about the modernity of humans. Although the find was announced in 1797 at a meeting of the Society of Antiquaries in London and an illustrated account of it was published in the society's journal in 1800, nobody seems to have paid much attention to it at the time. The author was John Frere (1740–1807), a gentleman and antiquarian who lived in Suffolk and he, at least, was well aware of the significance of what he was describing – a flint clearly worked by human hand into an axe.

Decent building stone is notably absent from the relatively young rock strata of the East Anglian region of England, and other materials – such as timber and bricks – have traditionally been used for most buildings. Clays suitable for brickmaking have been worked from surface deposits for centuries, and it was from such a digging near Hoxne in Suffolk in the late 1700s that workmen uncovered some curiously shaped flints. News of the find reached

Frere. He visited the site and made careful notes of the layering of the sands, clays and gravels, and marked the position of the stones within the succession. The bones of some of the extinct beasts of the Ice Age had been found in similar deposits nearby.

The flints included a very fine hand-sized and flat, pear-shaped specimen which had been clearly worked into a double-edged (bifaced) and sharply pointed axe. The shape is so well formed that Frere correctly concluded that it must have been 'fabricated and used by a people who had not the use of metals...'. He also noted that since it had been found buried within deposits well below the surface of the ground 'the situation at which these weapons were found may tempt us to refer them to a very remote period indeed, even beyond that of the present world'.

This was the first time that any such observation had been published, and his beautiful illustration of the handaxe leaves no doubt that it was produced by the hand of 'man' in the remote past. At the time the near-surface deposits which contained the flint artifact were known as Diluvium and generally thought to have to have been laid down by the Mosaic Flood. Such sands, gravels and clays, which are not yet consolidated or 'petrified' into stone, often contain the bones of large mammals and these were interpreted as victims of the Flood.

Unfortunately it appears that nobody paid any attention to Frere's find or was convinced of its veracity. Several decades were to pass before any great breakthrough was made in the mapping of human prehistory. Some early finds are, however, worth mentioning, especially that of Paviland Cave in South Wales.

ABOVE:
John Frere's 1800 description and illustration of this flint handaxe was the first in the world to recognise prehistoric human activity contemporary with the extinct animals of the Ice Age

The 'Red Lady' of Paviland

Between 1822–3 the Reverend William Buckland excavated Goat's Hole Cave in Paviland, one of several caves in the Gower Peninsula. Paviland Cave is a natural opening in Carboniferous limestone and is today situated at the base of a steep sea cliff on the coast overlooking the Bristol Channel. Over 5,000 artefacts are known to have come from here but it is likely that many more were washed out of the cave by the sea in recent times. For much of the Ice Age, when sea levels were significantly lower, the cave looked out over a flat coastal plain some 2km (1¼ miles) wide, and an 8km (5-mile) long finger of land that stretched westwards into Carmarthen Bay. The cave not only provided a natural shelter but also an excellent vantagepoint for viewing the movement of game.

When Buckland excavated the cave the scientific method of archaeological excavation had not been developed, so there is no accurate information about the original layering of the cave deposits or the position of the numerous artefacts within the layers. What Buckland did find was a skeleton, buried in a shallow grave along with seashells, perforated as for a necklace or some other ornament, plus carved pieces of mammoth ivory, including bracelets and long thin rods or wands. Everything had been dusted over with a scattering of red ochre, so it was apparent that the body had been buried with some ceremony.

BELOW & RIGHT:
Early 19th-century exploration of caves was revealing fossils of extinct animals and humans, but all were still seen by scientists such as Buckland as evidence for the Flood

Although Buckland described the find accurately enough, he concluded that the corpse was that of a Welsh woman, whom he called the 'Red Lady'. He believed that she lived during the Roman occupation of Britain, and her kinsfolk must have made the artefacts from bone and ivory found in the cave. Anatomically the skeleton was perfectly modern, so there was no particular reason for Buckland to think that the 'Red Lady' had any great antiquity. We do now know that he got the sex wrong; 'she' was a young man aged about 25, some 1.7m (5ft 6in) tall.

However, Buckland's convoluted explanation for the manufacture of the burial goods suggests that he was actively avoiding the simplest explanation for the age of the burial: that this young man lived and died at a time when extinct Ice Age animals were alive in the British Isles. His remains have been dated at around 26,350 +/-550 years old and so it is not surprising that he is an anatomically modern human. He was one of the Cro-Magnon people, hunters who migrated into Western Europe around 40,000 years ago. Some of them took advantage of the lowered sea levels to cross on dry land into Britain, only to be isolated when sea levels rose again. But none of this information was available to Buckland.

In retrospect Paviland is of considerable importance and interest, especially within the history of British archaeology. It is the richest of all the Welsh Palaeolithic (Stone

Age) sites and the only known ceremonial burial of Early Upper Palaeolithic age in the British Isles. The total collection of artefacts includes tools made of flint, chert, bone and antler. Some of the stone tools are dated around 28–30,000 years old and a bone spatula is some 23,670 years old, suggesting that the cave was intermittently occupied over a considerable period of time. By 23,000 years ago the very cold conditions of the glacial maximum brought glaciers and ice sheets down to the Gower Peninsula and probably led to the abandonment of Britain until recolonisation when the climate began to improve around 13,000 years ago.

Analysis of fossil bones from the cave shows that it was ideally sited for the human occupants to watch the movements of the Ice Age megafauna that were hunted for food, clothing and tools. These prey animals were mostly the kind of large plant-eating animals we associate with game parks in Africa today, such as deer (but reindeer here), bovids (bison), rhinoceros (woolly rhinoceros), elephant (woolly mammoth) and equids (horse), plus bears and less commonly giant deer, wolf and hyena.

Evidence from France

One of the positive legacies of the French Revolution was that some French intellectuals and scientists felt free enough to pursue an active interest in the possibilities of human prehistory. When Cuvier's colleague, the vertebrate palaeontologist Etienne Geoffroy St-Hilaire (1772–1844), was alerted to the discovery of the first fossil remains of an ape, in Gascony in 1834, he claimed that it 'presaged a new era of humanitarian knowledge' and went on to argue that 'if fossil apes exist so must fossil humans'.

St-Hilaire was soon proved right by French prehistorians who were aided by an accident of geological history. The landscapes of the Low Countries of Belgium and France had suffered less scouring and erosive forces of the Ice Age than the landscapes of Britain and much of mainland Northern Europe. Exceptions in the latter areas were limestone caves, within which sediments and fossils were protected from the destructive forces of glaciation. Overall there was a much greater chance of fossil and archaeological materials accumulating and surviving in surface deposits on the landscapes of France and Southern Europe. With France's intellectual tradition and climate being particularly active in the 18th and early 19th centuries, more so than many of its southern neighbours, French prehistorians made much of the 'running' in archaeological discovery at that time.

A number of important early finds helped break down the barriers of prejudice that prevailed amongst most natural historians of the day. In the late 1830s/40s a young 'amateur' of antiquities, Jacques Boucher de Crèvecoeur de Perthes (1788–1868), who came from a wealthy family and was director of customs at Abbeville on the Somme in Picardy, amassed a collection of more than a thousand worked flints from the Somme river valley deposits around St Acheul. In 1846 he reported his findings to the French Academy of Sciences, but they were rejected by the eminent French geologist Elie de Beaumont (1798–1874). Fortunately de Perthes was undeterred and the following year published his findings in a magnificent illustrated volume. Entitled *Antiquités celtiques et ante diluviennes*, it contained detailed descriptions and illustrations of the distinctive, pear-shaped flints (which came to be known as Acheulian handaxes) and the fossils bones they were associated with.

De Perthes was an accomplished and persuasive writer, but he was also prone to uncritical flights of romantic fantasy especially about the origin of art. He fell into the common trap of claiming that certain curious anthropomorphic shaped stones had been worked by humans, whereas they had in fact been fashioned by natural processes. Museum curators constantly have to explain to visitors that many stones that look like fish, legs, heads and whatever are just accidents of weathering and erosion.

De Perthes was, however, correct in claiming that the association of flint tools and bones of extinct animals built on Frere's pioneering observations and provided the first convincing evidence that humans had lived alongside the great antediluvian animals such as the mammoth, straight-tusked elephant, rhinoceros and bison. Ten years later he published a second volume, which dealt with the objections that had been raised to his ideas. By now some British scientists had been persuaded by de Perthes's evidence, and around the same time important discoveries in France were being investigated by the other pioneers of French archaeology Edouard Lartet (1801–71) and his son Louis Lartet (1840–99).

In 1852 a French road worker in Aurignac, southern France, pulled a human bone out of a hillside rabbit hole. A trench dug into the hill revealed a cave entrance blocked by a limestone boulder behind which lay 17 skeletons. The remains were promptly reburied in the local cemetery because they looked like modern human skeletons. News of the find attracted Edouard Lartet. In 1860 he excavated the cave floor and found more isolated human bones along with those of extinct animals. But still the scholars of the day remained unconvinced.

Lartet père was a zoologist and is now best known for the discovery of the first fossil apes. In 1837 he described the fossil of an anthropoid ape from his native Gascony, whose bones resembled those of the modern gibbons of Southeast Asia. Later the fossil was named as *Pliopithecus antiquus*, meaning 'ancient – greater monkey'. Lartet argued that if such fossil apes could exist, so might fossil humans. *Pliopithecus antiquus* is now known to be of Miocene age and lived some 14 million years ago, well before the first human relatives. In 1856 Lartet described the lower jaw and teeth of another ape which he called *Dryopithecus* ('ape of the oaks'), which was closer to modern great apes in appearance. It has since been classified with the orang-utan in the family Ponginae within the superfamily Hominidae.

This important fossil is now known to be of late Miocene age and is some 7 or 8 million years old. However, in recent years a new skull of *Dryopithecus*, some 10 million years old, has been found in Hungary. Well preserved, this cranial fossil may well show closer hominine affinities, suggesting that it belongs in a group with the African great apes and humans. The implications of this are particularly interesting since it also suggests that there may have been an early evolutionary phase when the ancestors we share with the great apes migrated out of Africa and developed in Eurasia before their descendants subsequently migrated back to Africa 7 or 8 million years ago.

Bones from the Neanderthal

By the middle of the 19th century, creeping industrialisation and improvements in agriculture led to an increasing demand for limestone for use in the booming iron industry and as agricultural lime. Quarrymen around Germany's centres of industry on the Rhine, such as Düsseldorf, extracted good quality limestone wherever they could find it. The nearby River Düssel, a tributary to the Rhine, flows through what was the picturesque Neander Thal (valley), named after a 17th-century clergyman and composer, Johann Neumann (1650–80), whose Latinised name was Neander. The rocky outcrops of limestone along the valley are perforated with numerous caves.

In 1856 some of those quarrymen uncovered human-like bones in one of the caves known locally as the Feldhofer

Grotto. As they dug out the cave floor deposits they discovered a number of very well-preserved bones including a skull roof, some limb bones and part of a pelvis. The quarrymen were used to finding the occasional bones and skulls of cave bears and other extinct Ice Age creatures but thought these bones were sufficiently different to interest the local schoolmaster Johann Fuhlrott, known to be fascinated by anything old.

Fuhlrott, although a complete amateur, was well read and recognised that the skullcap had very prominent bony eyebrow ridges and a very low sloping forehead, just like the illustration of a gorilla skull he had recently seen (described by Richard Owen in 1848). The limb bones were curiously curved and thick-walled. Fuhlrott realised that the skeleton was incomplete and returned to the find site with the workmen to see if he could retrieve any more of the bones.

Unfortunately the grotto had been emptied of all the remaining deposits and fossils, but he did ascertain the circumstances of the find as best he could from the workmen. Most significantly, he discovered that the bones had been buried beneath at least 1.5m (5ft) of mud. In addition, his detailed examination of the bones revealed that, in places, they were covered with curious little moss-shaped growths of mineral, similar to those found on cave-bear bones.

This was sharp scientific observation. Fuhlrott did not know the true significance of what he was seeing but noted it nonetheless. In retrospect these mineral growths, known as dendrites, are an important clue to the considerable antiquity of the bones. Their development requires prolonged burial in sediment, periodically flushed through with mineral-bearing groundwater.

LEFT:
The remains of the original Neanderthal skeleton found in 1856 as displayed in the Bonn museum at the end of the 19th century

Fuhlrott was also interested in the new biological ideas of the time. The stir caused by the 1844 publication in Britain of the anonymous *Vestiges of Creation*, with its blatantly evolutionary message, had spread into Europe. It occurred to Fuhlrott that these skeletal remains might belong to some human ancestor, perhaps a 'missing link' between apes and modern humans. However, he did not feel sufficiently confident or academically qualified to describe the bones properly, so he enlisted the help of Hermann Schaaffhausen (1816–93), a professor of anatomy at the University of Bonn.

At the first opportunity, Schaaffhausen and Fuhlrott presented their information, ideas and conclusions to a meeting of the Lower Rhine Medical and Natural History Society in Bonn on 4 February 1857. Schaaffhausen described the bones in detail, mentioning their heavy build, which implied that their 'owner' had a muscular physique and physically demanding lifestyle. In their 1861 published report on the 'Neanderthaler' the bones were accurately illustrated with beautiful engravings.

When it came to interpreting the find and drawing conclusions, Schaaffhausen and Fuhlrott were faced with considerable problems. Darwin's *Origin of Species* had been published in 1859 and the two scientists were well aware of the active debate about the nature of the development of organisms through time and particularly the thorny question of the antiquity of mankind. Schaafhausen had written *On the Constancy and Transformation of Species*, in which he tentatively concluded that the fixedness or 'immutability of species', as he referred to it, 'is not proven'. This was a roundabout way of admitting that species may have changed through time, a sentiment that was still highly contentious.

Without an established prehistoric context for the 'Neanderthaler', Schaaffhausen and Fuhlrott had to fall back on vague historical chronicles and speculated that 'the human bones from the Neanderthal exceed all the rest in those peculiarities... which lead to the conclusion of their belonging to a barbarous and savage race'. They also thought that such races may have 'coexisted with the animals found in the "Diluvium"'.

In many ways Schaaffhausen and Fuhlrott were right. The Neanderthaler did belong to an ancient group of humans that lived alongside the extinct animals of the 'Diluvium', now known as deposits associated with the Ice Age rather than the Flood. In addition, Schaaffhausen had not been able to resist the temptation to add a sprinkling of his 'proto-evolutionary' thoughts about the possibility of species improving through time: 'many a barbarous race may... have disappeared, together with the animals of the ancient world, whilst the races whose organisation is improved have continued the genus'. Reconstruction of the Neanderthaler's life and death was to get even more bizarre before he eventually found his rightful place in the human family 'tree'.

'Barbarity' and 'savagery' had become an integral part of the Neanderthaler's personal profile and it is only in recent years that this image has been questioned. It was normal for the scientists of the day to construe all but the most civilised humans in this way. Most scientists ascribed to a sliding scale of superiority and inferiority for living peoples and extended it to most historic and consequently all prehistoric peoples as they were discovered.

Again, in modern terms Schaaffhausen and Fuhlrott were not so far off the mark, but such comments were highly controversial at the time and unleashed a storm of criticism. August Mayer, a pathologist, and one of Schaaffhausen's faculty colleagues in Bonn, also examined the bones. He felt that the curved thigh bones were typical of a lifelong horseman, or could have been produced by rickets, a chronic nutritional deficiency disease of childhood due to a dietary lack of vitamin D or calcium. The condition was common amongst poor and undernourished children in 19th-century Europe. Mayer also pointed out that the Neanderthaler's left elbow had been fractured during life and had healed badly. He surmised that the prolonged pain of this injury – inducing constant frowning – had induced the furrowed browridge.

In putting all his observations together in 1864, Mayer attempted to explain away the unusual features of the skeleton within an everyday historic context. Thus Mayer, like Buckland, could not see what he was looking at and preferred the fanciful explanation that the bones belonged to a Cossack cavalryman whose regiment had been pursuing Napoleon's army as it retreated through Prussia. The Cossack had been injured in a skirmish and deserted when his regiment paused near the Rhine before pushing on into France in January 1814. On spotting the Feldhofer Grotto as a possible refuge, the cavalryman crawled into it, and eventually died there.

Professor Mayer's story is certainly good on imagination, but not so good as a scientific explanation of the Neanderthaler's peculiar osteology. Some historians of science think that there may well have been a hidden agenda behind his explanation. The dominant figure in German biological science at the time was Rudolf Virchow (1821–1902), a brilliant scientist who pioneered the study of cellular pathology, first described leukaemia, and had an interest in the developing science of archaeology. Perhaps unsurprisingly considering his background, Virchow supported Mayer's interpretation of the Neanderthaler's peculiar condition as pathological.

Virchow was also a politically active liberal, who remarked that 'there can be no scientific dispute with respect to faith, for science and faith exclude one another' but, nevertheless, he was also implacably opposed to the idea of evolution. Mayer

knew this and may have been keen to counter Fuhlrott's progressionist ideas in order to get the eminent Virchow's endorsement for his own interpretation of the find – and it worked.

The whole question of the status of the original Neanderthal remains may well have been forgotten or at least relegated to a very obscure footnote in academic books. However, a few British scientists were aware of the debate in Germany and they effectively rescued the Neanderthaler from obscurity.

Whilst the German scientists became bogged down in somewhat fruitless argument, Schaaffhausen's work was receiving a more enthusiastic reception in England. Although very few experts were prepared to countenance human antiquity, some very eminent ones – such as Charles Lyell, Thomas Henry Huxley (1825–95) and Charles Darwin (1809–82) – were. Darwin was as cautious as he could be about the implications of the Darwin/Wallace theory of evolution for human ancestry. The only comment he made about it in *The Origin of Species* was a rather throwaway concluding one-liner in which he suggests that 'Light will be thrown on the origin of man and his history'. But even this mild proposition was like a red rag to some fundamentalists. Huxley, however, was bolder and in 1863 published a collection of essays entitled

LEFT:
Thomas Henry Huxley (1825–95) who, in 1863, was one of the first scientists to argue that the theory of evolution applied to humans

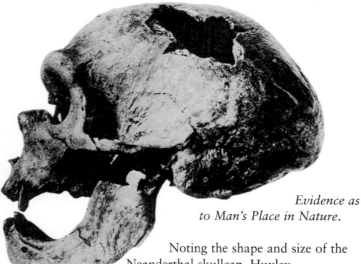

Evidence as to Man's Place in Nature.

Noting the shape and size of the Neanderthal skullcap, Huxley commented that it was 'the most pithecoid [ape-like] of known human skulls' belonging to the 'extreme term of a series leading gradually from it to the highest and best developed of human crania'. He questioned whether 'in still older strata do the fossilised bones of an Ape more anthropoid, or a man more pithecoid, than any yet known await the researches of some unborn palaeontologist?'

In the same year the Neanderthal fossils were finally recognised for what they truly are: the bones of an extinct species of human. The fossil was named *Homo neanderthalensis* by William King (1809–86), professor of geology in Galway, Ireland. His was the first acknowledgement that *Homo sapiens* had extinct but still human relatives. Nevertheless, it still took time before King's new human species was generally accepted.

We know now that the Neanderthals occupied much of Europe from North Wales south to Gibraltar, eastwards to the Levant (the region around today's Israel and Lebanon) and north to the Caucasus. The Neanderthals evolved from an even older human relative, *Homo heidelbergensis*, perhaps well over 400,000 years ago. Isotopic analysis of their bones has shown that they were 'serious' meat eaters who hunted a range of game from tortoises to mammoths. They survived through the dramatically fluctuating climate changes of the latter part of the Quaternary Ice Age until around 28,000 years ago when they became extinct. Their last 12,000 years were encroached upon by modern humans, *Homo sapiens*, who first moved out of Africa around 150,000 years ago. Surprisingly perhaps, despite the overlap, recent analysis of Neanderthal DNA suggests that the two peoples did not interbreed to any significant extent.

DNA forensic evidence

In 1997 scientists were able to recover and analyse fossil DNA from some Neanderthal bones. The genetic material was successfully extracted from the bone of that specimen of *Homo neanderthalensis* found in 1856 in the Neander Valley. Detailed comparison shows that the difference between Neanderthal and modern human DNA was three times greater than differences found within the whole range of modern humans, but it was only half the measure of difference between modern humans and chimps.

The size of the human-Neanderthal genetic difference suggests that the two groups must have diverged a considerable time ago, estimated at between 555,000 and 690,000 years, according to the molecular clock. As there appears to be no persisting genetic signature of any interbreeding, it would seem that the Neanderthals and modern humans kept apart. They may have been genetically distant but there is good evidence that geographically some of them lived within sight of one another.

Update

In 1997 Ralf Schmitz and Jürgen Thissen, two German archaeologists, managed to locate the original dump of sediment dug out of the Feldhofer Grotto in 1856. The debris was still lying at the bottom of the cliff and had been protected over the intevening 140 years by a covering of scree fragments of limestone. During a careful search of the sediment, Schmitz and Thissen were amazed to find stone tools along with animal and 20 human-related pieces of bone. The latter included fragments which could be fitted to the original skeleton and bits of another right thigh bone showing that originally there must have been more than one skeleton in the cave. The animal bones have cut marks from stone tools suggesting that they had been butchered by the Neanderthals. Carbon dating of the bones gives a radiocarbon age of about 40,000 years.

Chapter 4
Carving up the past

'Strata Smith' and the making of geological maps

Although the arguments about the organic nature of fossils had largely been resolved by the late 18th century, fossils were still generally viewed apart from the geological rock context within which they were found. The general localities from which particular fossils came might be known, but these were just indicative of the local geography rather than giving a four-dimensional setting of local geology and time framework. However, there was a growing awareness amongst naturalists (such as John Woodward and Robert Hooke – 1635–1703) that strata often had distinctive features that related back to the circumstances within which they were originally deposited. In addition, particular sedimentary strata often contained distinctive types of fossils. But the circumstances of deposition of those sediments and the fossil content of the strata were still essentially connected to the events of the Deluge.

It was becoming evident that the geographical distribution of strata and their contained fossils had this complex dimensional context. There were the three dimensions of landscape topography beneath which the strata lay, within which there was this fourth temporal dimension represented by the prehistoric depositional succession of strata and fossils. Previously

the distribution of geological strata outcropping across landscapes had not been mapped out in any consistent fashion. What few geological maps there were tended to show how rocks occurred at the surface in certain small regions of Europe. Few gave any indication of how the strata related to one another at depth. Some pioneering attempts to depict this had been made, especially in mining regions in Germany such as Thuringia. Georg Füschel's (1722–73) remarkable 1761 map of part of Thuringia gives an oblique bird's-eye view

BELOW:
Georg Fuchsel's pioneering 1761 geological map shows the distribution of strata across the Thuringian hills

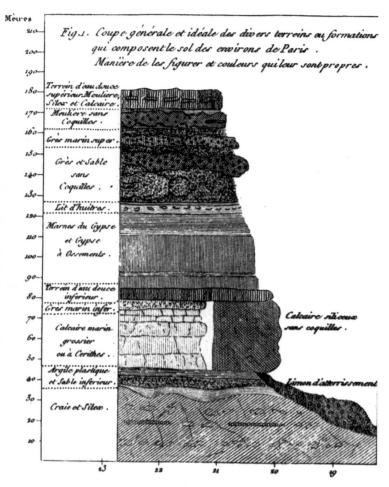

ABOVE:
A generalised vertical section through the sequence of strata in the Paris Basin as measured by Georges Cuvier and Alexandre Brongniart

ABOVE RIGHT:
Part of Cuvier and Brongniart's geological map of the Paris Basin, published in 1811, showing the disposition of the strata seen in the section

of how the topography related to the underlying strata with their geological structure shown in a vertical cross-section.

The need for better geological maps increased with changing land use from the end of the 18th century into the 19th. The Agricultural Revolution produced the need for better transport systems, especially canals that could carry bulk agricultural produce cheaply. These had to cut across varied terrains with largely unknown geology. Subsequently the Industrial Revolution brought a rapidly increasing demand for geological materials such as coal, iron ore, stone and clay. These were required for the building of the next generation of transport systems, the railways and 'metalled' roads that also required many new bridges and supporting infrastructures. For the first time land owners and speculators wanted to know what kind of rocks and valuable natural resources lay hidden beneath the surface. The only way they could find out was by having their lands mapped and surveyed by

the new breed of professional geological surveyors. To predict what strata lay hidden beneath so much of the British landscape with its thick soils, crops and woodlands, it was necessary to understand the underground geometry of strata. That could only be worked out once there was a proper understanding of the succession of strata and how they were structurally arranged within the Earth.

The so-called stratigraphic method of geological mapping was independently discovered in both France and England. In France Georges Cuvier and Alexandre Brongniart pioneered its use in mapping the distribution of strata across the Paris Basin in 1811. In England William Smith, an English surveyor and canal engineer, also developed the method.

Smith was the orphaned son of an Oxfordshire blacksmith whose humble rural social background and training was very different from that of most geologists of the time. The emerging science was predominantly in the hands of either university-based academics or financially independent gentlemen of metropolitan science, and a small but growing circle of middle-class geologists who were looking for employment in the museums, institutes and surveys that were being developed to house the new science. Smith's social and educational background effectively placed him 'beyond the pale' of scientific geology; but his technical achievement in the development of geological mapping, with the use of characteristic fossils, was on a par with the achievements of the other great British technologists of the age such as the Stephensons (George and Robert) or the Brunels (Marc and Isambard). Their work is well known; by comparison, William Smith and his work has barely been revealed until very recently, outside the relatively small world of geologists and historians of science.

Wherever his work as a surveyor took him, Smith grasped the opportunity to directly observe the succession of strata (layers of ancient sediment turned to stone within the Earth), their physical character and fossil content. He went underground, down mines, into muddy canal cuts and dangerous quarries. Very few of the gentlemen geologists had such valuable first-hand experience and probably would not have wanted to. From his childhood in Oxfordshire, Smith learned the local names and properties of the economically useful 'seams' of building stone, such as the 'Oolite and Ragstone' and clay layers such as 'Fuller's Earth'. Like many rural children in this part of England, with its low rolling hills and vales following the dry limestone escarpments and wet clay river valleys, he was also familiar with the common fossils of the local strata such as shepherd's crowns (sea urchins) and snakestones (ammonites). They often turned up as fields were ploughed and stone was quarried for lime and building.

Smith could speak the language of quarrymen and miners. By building on the experience of generations of artisans, who passed on their hard-won experience and observation by word of mouth, he was able to glean a vast amount of information that was not available in the academic literature of the time. Perhaps Smith's greatest disadvantage was that he had little talent for presenting his information and observations in the particular technical mode that middle-class form required; or perhaps it was just that he was not educated in this mode of communication. His great talent was for visually communicating information about strata in the form of beautiful and sophisticated maps. Whilst striking with their multi-coloured stripes and patches, such maps require a lot of interpretation and can be very puzzling, if not incomprehensible to the untutored, even today.

With the rapid expansion of the canal network came a new opportunity. Economics required accurate prediction of the rock substrata and knowledge of the availability of suitable local rock materials, stone for locks, bridges, aqueducts and clay to 'puddle' (provide a watertight

BELOW:
William Smith's excellent 1816 illustrations of the fossils (molluscs 1–6, brachiopods 7–8 and shark's teeth 9) typically found in the Cretaceous Chalk and regarded by him as diagnostic of this horizon

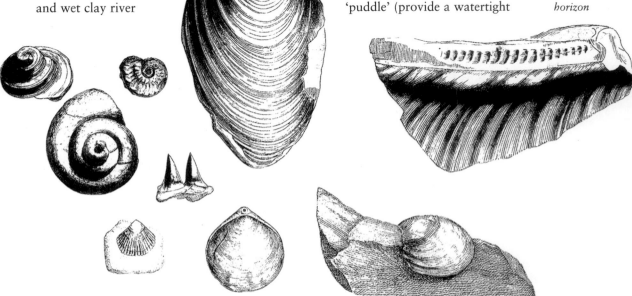

dating of strata. As Smith traced lines of hills with their outcrops of rock strata across the countryside he saw and measured how they had been tilted by earth movements and was able to match sequences of strata which appeared in different places. Although the overall succession of strata was already known in outline, especially that of the younger horizons which occur in the south-east of England, Smith found he was able to fill in the details and make new connections between strata of similar age in different parts of the country.

By 1801 Smith had traced the outcrop of Jurassic age strata from the coast around Whitby through the North York Moors south-west along the Cotswold scarps to the Dorset coast. He then extended his geological mapping across southern England where most of the 'Secondary' strata (now called Mesozoic) are, but gently inclined. Like the younger 'Tertiary' strata of the Paris Basin, they have relatively simple geological structure in the way of folds and faults. In 1815 Smith was in a position to publish his great map entitled *A Delineation of the Strata of England and Wales with part of Scotland*. There was an accompanying descriptive memoir but Smith did not find it easy to promote his work in writing, although he wrote a good deal in his journals. His map of England and Wales is the earliest detailed geological map in the world of such a large area and at such a scale (5 miles to 1in). For a largely individual effort, it was a remarkable achievement by any standard.

The compilation of these maps also produced a generalised stratigraphic column of the succession of strata. It extended from the youngest 'Diluvium' (Holocene and Pleistocene in age) at the top, down to the oldest undifferentiated 'Grauwacke' strata of Wales (Silurian, Ordovician and Cambrian in age). The sequence of strata was illustrated by a vertical section from London to Snowdon. The older rocks in south-west England, Wales and Scotland were still much less well known and Smith's excursions into these wilder and more complex geological terrains were brief; consequently their rocks are only sketchily shown on his map.

Smith freely showed his maps to anyone

lining) for the canal. With his unique combination of surveying skills and deep knowledge of the properties of the various strata, Smith was the right man in the right place, both to be employed in these endeavours and to gain more knowledge from what was being revealed by the new canal cuts that itinerant bands of 'navigators' were slicing through the British landscape.

Like his French contemporaries Cuvier and Brongniart, Smith realised that certain types of fossils only occurred at particular levels in the layers of strata. By 1799 Smith had drawn up the first tabulation of the succession of strata in the west of England. Through the identification of the various rock types and their contained fossils, it was possible to predict what strata should be found above and below any given layer.

Fossils were shown to have a fundamental importance for the relative who was interested and somewhat injudiciously let them be copied. The Geological Society of London had been founded in 1807, effectively as a private dining club for well-to-do gentlemen interested in debating geological matters. Being a mere surveyor without much formal education, Smith was not invited to join even though he was well known to some of the founding members. Smith was not seen as a gentleman, something of which he was painfully aware, noting in his diary that 'the theory of geology is in the possession of one class of men, the practice in another'. He was firmly in the latter class.

Worse still, the gentlemen of the Society set about making their own map which would use Smith's hard-won information and compete with his great map. The Geological Society's map was published in 1819 and resulted in a serious loss of sales for Smith, even though he had over 400 subscribers. That, plus a disastrous investment, caused him to run into such financial difficulties that in the same year he was committed to the King's Bench Prison in Southwark for a debt of some £300. Landing in debtors' gaol was not uncommon: the engineer Marc Brunel (1769–1849), father of the even more famous engineer Isambard Kingdom Brunel (1806–59), was similarly imprisoned, yet was discharged and subsequently knighted.

Nevertheless Smith was financially ruined and his wife's mental health was deteriorating. On release from prison he returned to working as a surveyor and land steward in the north of England. Fortunately his employer and benefactor, Sir John Johnstone, was a man of influence as member of parliament and fellow of the Geological Society. Gradually, through Johnstone's help and that of a network of up-and-coming geologists who realised just what he had achieved, Smith's reputation was rehabilitated within the Society – but not until nine years after his release.

Why exactly the grandees of the Geological Society such as Lyell, Murchison and Sedgwick decided to promote Smith when they did is an interesting question. Was it perhaps anything to do with competing claims for innovation in geological mapping that were coming from abroad? The French, after all, had the

justifiable claim that the already internationally famous Cuvier had 'invented' the geological map, whilst all Britain could produce was an unknown surveyor who had not even been accepted into the ranks of the Geological Society.

William Smith's public rehabilitation can be traced back to volume one of Charles Lyell's *Principles of Geology* (1830), the book Darwin took on the *Beagle* voyage as his geological 'bible'. Lyell praises Smith's 1790 *Tabular View of the British Strata* in which he had arrived at 'the laws of superposition of stratified rocks; that he was aware that the order of succession of different groups (of strata) was never inverted; and that they might be identified at very distant points by their peculiar organized fossils'. Furthermore, Smith 'laboured to construct a geological map of the whole of England; and with the greatest disinterestedness of mind, communicated the results of his investigations to all who desired information, giving such publicity to his original views, as to enable his contemporaries almost to compete with him in the race'. The latter is a diplomatic gloss and partial admission of the role played by the previous 'worthies' of the Society who had 'ripped off' Smith's data for their own

ABOVE:
Charles Lyell, whose 1830 Principles of Geology *helped to re-establish the reputation of William Smith and his achievements in the world of geology*

ABOVE:
*William Smith
(1769–1839), a largely
self-taught technical
genius and pioneer in
geological surveying and
mapmaking*

University of Cambridge and president of the Geological Society, felt 'compelled... to perform this act of filial duty... and to place our first honour on the brow of The Father of English Geology... he that gave the plan, and laid the foundations, and erected a portion of the solid walls, by the unassisted labour of his hands'. The title 'The Father of English Geology' has stuck ever since. Most biographical dictionaries of science and introductory texts to geology pay similar obeisance to William Smith as 'the real founder of stratigraphical geology' (*The Concise Dictionary of National Biography*, 1903), 'Today considered to be the "Father of English geology"' (*The Cambridge Dictionary of Scientists*, 1996).

Even the eminent German geologist, Karl Alfred von Zittel, in his *History of Geology and Palaeontology* (1899), joined in the hagiography, although in a somewhat more sober tone, remarking that 'Smith confined himself to the empirical investigation of his country, and was never tempted into general speculations about the history of formation of the earth. His greatness is based upon this wise restraint and the steady adherence to his definite purpose; to these qualities, the modest, self-sacrificing, and open-hearted student of nature owes his well-deserved reputation as the "Father of English Geology"'.

The only degree William Smith was awarded was an honorary doctorate from the University of Dublin, Trinity College in 1836, along with Louis Agassiz, the Swiss palaeontologist, when the British Association for the Advancement of Science was held in the city. Perhaps Smith's award was helped along by his nephew John Phillips (1800–74), who was assistant secretary of the Association at the time and who subsequently became professor of geology at Trinity from 1844–53, when he wrote one of the few accounts of Smith's professional life (1844). Like Smith, Phillips had been orphaned as a child and was adopted by his uncle William, from whom he had acquired his interest and basic tutoring in geology.

Perhaps some aspects of Smith's life deterred would-be biographers – such as his imprisonment for debt and his wife's madness – the sort of things that are almost essential for such a biography today. Even

map. There is, of course, no mention of the calamitous results for Smith personally.

Lyell goes on to describe Smith's map as 'a lasting monument of original talent and extraordinary perseverance... (who) had succeeded in throwing into natural divisions the whole complicated series of British rocks' and quotes one of the great German mineralogist Abraham Gottlob Werner's students, D'Aubuisson, as remarking in 1819 that 'what many celebrated mineralogists had only accomplished for a small part of Germany in the course of half a century, had been effected by a single individual for the whole of England'. Clearly, with Lyell's 1830 publication and such praise Smith's rehabilitation was well under way – Lyell had also compared him to Werner himself – and in 1831 Smith was awarded the new prestigious medal of the Geological Society of London, the Wollaston Gold Medal.

In his encomium Adam Sedgwick, Woodwardian professor of geology in the so, one might have thought that the 19th century would have thrown up a biography with its promotion of 'self-made men' such as the Scots stonemason Hugh Miller and Robert Dick, baker of Thurso, both of whom were deeply involved in geological discoveries and debates and were duly 'canonised' for it. Curiously Samuel Smiles (1812–1904), the guru of self-help, did mention Smith in his famous book *Self-Help* (1859), but went on to write a full biography of Dick, rather than Smith, and a three-volume work on the *Lives of the Engineers* (1861–2) which helped promote the likes of the Stephensons and Brunels.

Smith's pioneering work and his great technical achievement were stimulated by the development of the Industrial Revolution. He earned his living as a professional civil engineer making land evaluations, topographical and geological surveys both above and below ground. One of the main driving factors which led so many land owners and new companies to commission such surveys at the time was the huge growth in demand for canal building and the underground search for that 'black gold' – coal. Made of compressed plant material that had originally taken millions of years to grow in ancient tropical forests, coal was the fossil fuel that literally fed the fires of the Industrial Revolution. Within the British Isles and much of Western Europe the economic reserves of this fossil fuel were mostly burned up within less than 200 years. The geological understanding of the nature of plant fossils was just as slow in developing as that of animal fossils.

Discovering plant fossils

Plant fossils are generally rare in sedimentary rocks because most strata preserved in the rock record are the seabed deposits of shallow seas. However, coal is made of compressed plant material and so plants must be common in certain rock layers, especially those associated with what we know as the Carboniferous Coal Measures today. Since strata of this age outcrop in parts of the British Isles, North-western Europe and North America, large numbers of plant fossils were found as soon as the coal deposits began to be exploited

CL. III. Lithophyta

188 *189*

Tab. 4.

commercially as the Industrial Revolution got under way. The discovery in the first decades of the 19th century of plant fossils associated with coal deposits provided evidence of abundant and evidently luxuriant growth of ferns and other strange tree-sized plants during Carboniferous times. They also provided some of the first evidence that global climates had perhaps changed dramatically through geological time. However, some of the earliest discoveries of fossil plants date back to the later part of the 17th century when the nature of fossils was still being debated.

Edward Lhwyd was a well-known scholar and explorer of the highways and byways of rural Britain. He was curious about almost everything to do with the past as well as with the living organisms of the natural world. Lhwyd was not convinced by either the organic or inorganic theories for the origin of fossils and proposed a 'middle way'. In a book published in 1699 he illustrated a selection of fossil ferns and insects from Coal Measure (Carboniferous) strata, but was particularly intrigued by the appearance and origin of the ferns. The

197

puzzle was that they looked so plant-like but were not preserved with any plant-like material; they were just impressions of fronds on the rock surface; and they were not quite like any known living plant. Lhwyd concluded that the fossils must have grown within rock strata from 'seed' (pollen) that had percolated into the rocks from living plants which they most resembled. Johann Scheuchzer still had the same problem with fossil plants when he published his *Herbarium of the Deluge* in 1709, as he illustrated some inorganic mineral dendrites alongside what can be seen today as genuine fossil plants. As Scheuchzer's title suggests, the preservation of plant-like fossils in rock strata far inland was the result of the Noachian Deluge.

The famous diarist John Evelyn (1620–1706) had first reported the existence of plant-related fossils from the London Clay, which is of Eocene age (some 50 million years old) in 1668. Since then, some 300 species and 35 genera of fossil plant have been described from the Isle of Sheppey in the Thames Estuary. The proximity of these fossil-bearing deposits to London meant that many gentlemen collectors who were generally interested in natural 'curios' came to hear about them. Networks of working-class locals, especially women and children, searched out specimens, commonly known as 'figs' because of their brown wrinkled appearance, on the muddy and often fog-swathed foreshores. Prize specimens were fed through dealers and middlemen to the people who were prepared to pay for them. Most of the fossils are the mineralised seeds of flowering plants, with the teeth of many different kinds of sharks, bony fish, reptiles along with bits of turtle and so on.

In 1757 James Parsons (1705–70) described and illustrated some of the fossil seeds including striking specimens of the palm fruits *Nypa*. He declared that because of the evident ripeness of the fruits, the Flood must have overwhelmed the plants in autumn. By the end of the 18th century, Francis Crow had amassed such a collection of the fossils over a 20-year period that in 1810 he was able to describe 100 species. From his diagnosis of their taxonomic affinities he concluded that they once belonged to a tropical or high southern latitude vegetation. This was one of the first connections to be made between fossil plants and ancient climates – and a remarkably accurate one at that.

The tradition of collecting at Sheppey, still some five hours away from London even by steam packet, continued throughout the 19th century. In 1840 James Bowerbank, a city businessman, published a *History of the fossil Fruits and Seeds of the London Clay*, which was the first descriptive catalogue of the flora. Bowerbank also instructed would-be collectors how to penetrate the Dickensian world of the fossickers such as 'a woman

OPPOSITE & THIS PAGE:
Edward Lhwyd's 1699 illustrations of plant and insect fossils from coal deposits now known to be Carboniferous in age

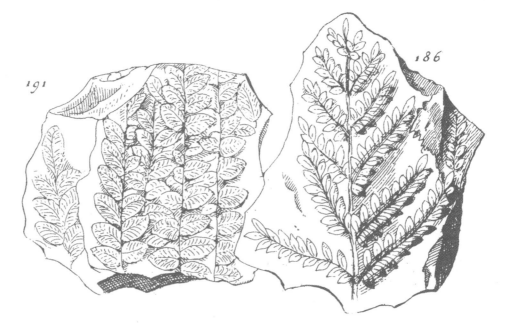

named Mummery, and several others who work upon the beach... these people will direct the traveller to the cottage of a family named Crockford... [who] will direct our fossil-hunter to many other parties who also work upon the beach... At Hensbrook enquiry should be made for a man named Pead... from this point... he must enquire for Mud Row, many of the inhabitants of which work upon the beach'.

A recent summary of this diverse fossil vegetation of 50 million years ago shows that it represents a lush coastal paratropical broadleaf forest that included tropical families such as sumac, custard apple, palm, dogwood and frankincense, and was inhabited by newly evolving mammals such as dog-sized primitive horses. The nearby warm shallow sea teemed with fish, turtles and crocodiles.

The trouble with plant fossils

There was a particular problem with trying to study fossil plants that resulted from the way they are recruited to the fossil record. Very rarely does a complete plant, from the extremities of its roots to its leaf tips and reproductive structures, get preserved in its entirety in the rock record. That would require the plant to be uprooted and instantly buried in sediment – not impossible, but nearly so. Normally life-and-death processes separate out the various parts of plants and bury them at different times in different places.

Rarely, in fossil forest or swamp-like situations such as the Coal Measure deposits, tree-sized trunks with their roots may be preserved still standing upright; but the rest of the canopy cannot be preserved intact. Branches, leaf fronds and reproductive structures might be found in the surrounding sediment, but there is no guarantee which root and trunk they originally belonged to. Leaf fronds may be blown from plants and carried some distance by wind and water along with other light plant components, especially pollen. Flowers are particularly delicate structures and very difficult to fossilise, although seeds, nuts and fruit can be much tougher.

They generally become separated from the parent plant and buried in fine sediment such as lake or river muds along with pollen and other buoyant plant debris. But these processes tend to mix up pieces from many different plants. As early investigators found, it can be very difficult to reassemble the parent plant from the fossil fragments. Just to confuse matters each different fossilised plant element was given its own name. So a leaf frond might be placed in one species, its stem in another, and so on.

LEFT:
Fossils from the London Clay, including the subtropical palm Nipa

Discovering plant prehistory

One of the most important of the early 19th-century studies of fossil plants was made by the French naturalist, Adolphe Brongniart (1801–76), son of Cuvier's collaborator Alexandre Brongniart. In his 1828 pioneering book on fossil plants *Histoire des Végétaux Fossile*, Brongniart *fils* concluded that there had been four distinct phases in the prehistory of plants, within each of which there had been gradual change. These gradual phases were, however, separated by abrupt breaks. The first phase was dominated by the primitive land plants of the Coal Measures; the second contained the first conifers; cycads appeared in the third (Mesozoic) phase and along with the conifers dominated the flora;

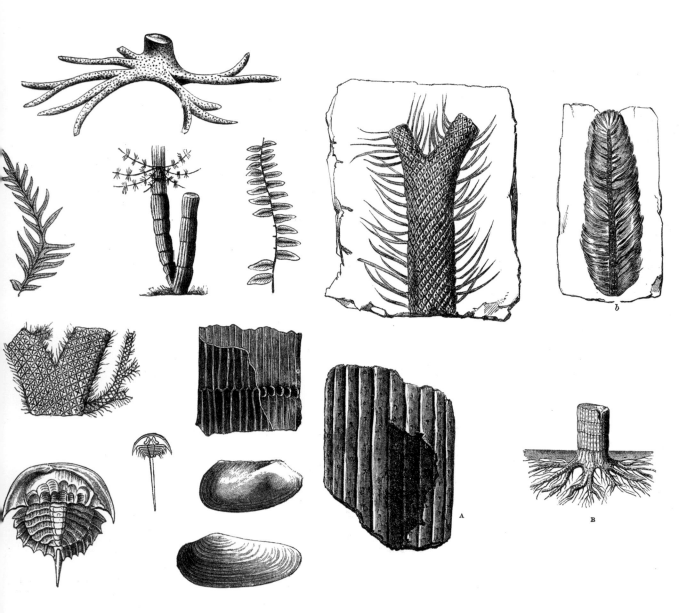

finally the flowering plants took over (Cainozoic). Altogether, to Brongniart, this represented a progressive history of increasing complexity and diversity similar to that which seemed to be emerging from the fossil record of animal life.

Brongniart also discerned another important feature of the plant fossil record. The fossil plants of the first phase, the luxuriant fossil tree-ferns, clubmosses and horsetails, although extinct, showed characters similar to plants that grow only in hot humid tropical rainforests today. He concluded that the global climate of the Earth must have been significantly warmer than that of today, since tropical warmth extended as far north as regions of North-western Europe (such as Scotland, from

where such fossil plants had been found). We now know that there are other explanations for this phenomenon (see below), but at the time it was an important breakthrough which resurrected Buffon's theory of a cooling Earth.

Even more ahead of its time was Brongniart's proposal that the abundance of plants during Coal Measure times was an indication of high levels of carbon dioxide in the atmosphere. Moreover, the effect of abundant plant life was to lock up carbon from the atmosphere in coal deposits and consequently CO_2 levels and global temperatures rose sufficiently to allow air-breathing reptiles to thrive. We now know that he was basically correct. Atmospheric CO_2 levels were perhaps ten times higher than present in Devonian times (around 600ppm). However, as terrestrial vegetation flourished through the Carboniferous Period it 'drew down' CO_2 from the atmosphere and locked it up in the plants. The accumulated debris from the plants was so extensive and voluminous that it built up thick layers in places, which in turn were buried and compressed over time to form coal deposits. There was so much vegetation globally that atmospheric CO_2 was reduced close to that of today at around 354ppm, drastically cooling global climates from their Devonian high point. This ice-house climate state precipitated an ice age from the end of Carboniferous times into the Permian Period. In the equatorial regions climates became drier and the rainforest cover was drastically reduced, although coal deposits were still formed in China in early Permian times.

Today's global distribution of Carboniferous coal-bearing rocks can be explained by plate tectonics. When the coal-rich parts of the continents are reassembled, as they were in Carboniferous times, they all fall within an equatorial belt from Arkansas and Kansas in central North America, through the Maritime Provinces of Canada, North-western Europe (British Isles, northern Germany, Netherlands, Belgium, northern France and Poland) and extend across to the Ukraine and China.

The plants the dinosaurs ate

In the late 1820s John Phillips, William Smith's nephew, was gathering information for his pioneering book on the geology of the Yorkshire coast. The coastal strata are often well exposed and in places highly fossiliferous, a fact known to generations of locals. Like their counterparts at the other end of the country in Dorset, a network of local collectors and dealers was established as soon as money was to be made from the sale of fossils. Students of geology ranged from amateurs, often members of the local literary and philosophical societies that became fashionable in the latter decades of the 18th century and persisted into the early 19th. There were also the occasional but growing bands of professionals, mostly (but not always) university men and those who struggled to make a precarious living from surveying and map making, such as William Smith and his nephew.

By 1825 fossil plants had been found in

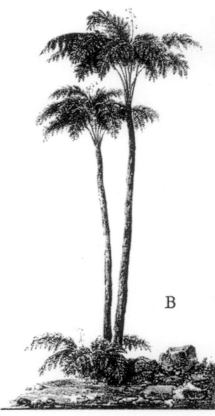

BELOW:
High latitude Coal Measure treefern fossils compared with a modern tropical treefern, from which Adolphe Brongniart concluded that the Earth had been hotter in Carboniferous times

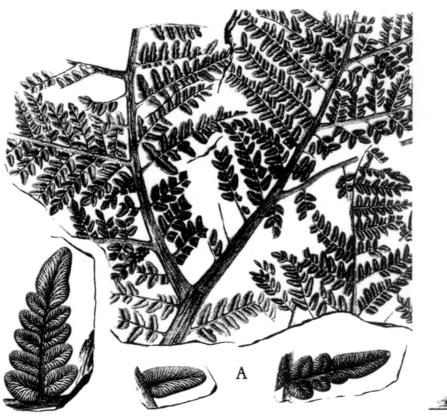

rocks of the Oolitic Period (later referred to as the Jurassic Period) at a number of localities on the Yorkshire coast north of Scarborough and Saltwick, south of Whitby. Specimens collected by locals were bought by societies such as that in York for their museums. Adolphe Brongniart, on his way to Scotland, was shown the collection of plants in York by John Phillips. In 1826 Roderick Murchison (1792–1871) arrived to view them and the coastal sections, from which they originated, in preparation for a trip to Sutherland in Scotland. There, on the northern shore of the Moray Firth in the village of Brora was a coal mine.

Coal at Brora had been exploited from surface exposures since 1529, and the first pit was dug in 1598. New mines had been opened in 1810 and Murchison wanted to see if the Brora coal strata were the same age as those of the Yorkshire oolites. Coal was mined sporadically from a number of small pits in Yorkshire strata of Jurassic age since 1648. Birdforth Colliery was the largest mine with a shaft 46m (150ft) deep sunk in 1760, but even at the height of its productivity it only employed some 30 men, and it closed in 1798. Murchison was always keen to try and apply geological knowledge to economic ends and subsequently made considerable efforts to deter landowners from wasting money searching for coal in rocks that would never yield any.

The 1827 discovery of fossil plants at Gristhorpe on the Yorkshire coast was to put the district firmly on the fossil collector's map. There was some dispute over who first discovered the fossil locality. Two local collectors who were cousins, William Bean and John Williamson, both claimed priority. Since then over 300 different plant species, many new to science, have been found in the Jurassic strata of the region. One third of these come from the strata exposed on the coast at Gristhorpe, now internationally recognised as the best locality in the world for fossil plants of this age. Brongniart named four new species after Williamson, and Bean's contribution was subsequently acknowledged by the naming of a cycad genus after him.

The modern interpretation of the deposit is that the plants were part of a diverse vegetation of bryophytes, clubmosses, ferns, caytonias, cycads, ginkgophytes, conifers and so on which grew around a lagoon. Bits of the plants were blown or fell into the lagoon where, over the years, they were buried and preserved in fine mud. Several fossil plants, such as the cycad *Beania* tree, have been reassembled from Gristhorpe fossils. The fossils were first brought to the attention of the wider geological community by John Phillips's 1829 book *Illustrations of the Geology of Yorkshire*. John Williamson's son, William Williamson (1816–95), provided many of the specimens, descriptions and drawings of the plants for Phillips's book. William Williamson later became professor of botany and geology at Queen's College in Manchester (later the University of Manchester) and effectively founded the academic study of fossil plants in Britain. A decade or so later it was realised that the remarkable fossil floras that had been preserved in these Jurassic strata were the

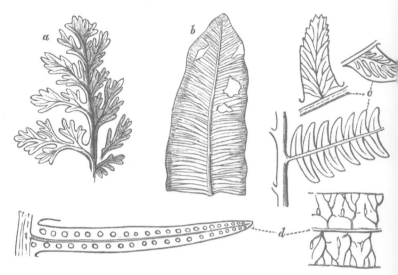

ABOVE:
Details of Jurassic fern fossils, including some named by Adolphe Brongniart from Yorkshire specimens

basic food supply of the dinosaur food chain, consumed by the innumerable herbivorous dinosaurs of all dimensions from ostrich-sized bipedal forms to the biggest land-living animals of all time, the giant sauropods.

A boundary dispute in the Welsh hills

The most commonly found fossils are shells of familiar marine creatures such as clams, snails, sea urchins and corals, which are still around in today's seas, along with extinct groups such as trilobites, ammonites, brachiopods and graptolites in older sedimentary rocks. Such fossils have made it possible to distinguish sequences of rock strata; realise how and where they were originally deposited; establish a general statigraphic succession or history of deposition of the strata; subdivide geological time; and correlate between separate surface outcrops of strata of similar age.

By the first decades of the 1800s, rock strata appearing at the Earth's surface had already been divided into Tertiary, Secondary and Primitive strata. These broad divisions were originally defined by mineralogists such as the German Johann Gottlob Lehmann in the 1760s. Primitive rocks were thought to have been first formed during the initial stages of the Earth's creation and were therefore devoid of fossil remains. These rocks included granites, schists and basalts, and were found in mountainous regions. Above lay the stratified Secondary deposits, found on the flanks of mountains and supposed to have been deposited during the Deluge, and so were full of the petrified remains of victims of the Flood. They included strata such as limestones, clayrocks and sandstones. Above these lay the Tertiary deposits, a younger group of fossiliferous sediments that formed low hills. Some of their materials were thought to have been derived from the erosion and redeposition of Secondary strata.

By the middle of the 18th century Giovanni Arduino (1713–95), an Italian professor of mineralogy in Padua University, had come to realise that the sequence seen in nature was not so straightforward. There were other categories of rocks, such as volcanic, which did not fit into such a simple scheme. Some rock types, such as limestone, could be found in both Secondary and Tertiary divisions. In 1787 a German mineralogist and highly influential teacher, Abraham Gottlob Werner (1749–1817), published a more advanced classification of rocks.

Above the Primitive rocks Werner recognised what he called Transition rocks. These were primarily seen as chemical precipitates of a global ocean but including some stratified deposits, produced by the erosion of Primitive rocks. Werner called

his version of Secondary strata *Flötz-Schichten* or stratified rocks, made up of fossiliferous sandstones, limestones, slates, coal and so on. Above these lay his *Aufgeschwemmte-Gebirge* or Alluvial strata (equivalent to the Tertiary deposits), formed by running water carrying eroded material from the land into the sea to form sands, peats and clays. In addition there were volcanic products, such as ash and cinder beds, all of which could be fossiliferous. To Werner, his four subdivisions reflected the history of the formation of the Earth's crust.

By the early decades of the 19th century many local and regional subdivisions of strata had been recognised and named, and were being mapped out by pioneers such as Georges Cuvier and Alexandre Brongniart in France and William Smith in England. Some distinctive suites of strata were already thought to be coeval over larger regions, such as the *Terrain Bituminifere* of Belgium, which was named in 1808 by the Belgian geologist Jean Baptiste Julien d'Omalius d'Halloy (1783–1875), who had been greatly influenced by the work of Cuvier and Brongniart. By 1822 d'Halloy had made a general survey of the major geological formations of the lowlands of France, Belgium and adjacent regions of

BELOW:
Johann Lehmann's 1756 geological cross-section through the Flötzgebirge or Secondary strata (of Permo-Triassic age) in Thuringia

Germany and Switzerland. His geological map, on a scale of 1 to 4 million, was first published in his *Text-book of Geology* in 1822. The same year saw the publication in Britain of the *Outlines of the Geology of England and Wales* by the Reverend Dean William Daniel Conybeare and William Phillips (1775–1828). The anglicised name Carboniferous was coined by these British authors for the period and has remained in international currency ever since.

As they wrote, 'the class of rocks thus constituted will contain not only the great coal-deposit itself, but those of limestone and sandstone also on which it reposes... the epithet Carboniferous is of obvious application to this series'. They thought that this Carboniferous System was distinct from both Werner's *Flötz-Schichten* and *Transition*, although, if anything, it was more allied to the latter than the former. The Carboniferous has since become an internationally recognised system of strata (but without the Old Red Sandstone) and represents the Carboniferous Period of geological time, which we now know lasted from 354 to 290 million years ago.

The early decades of the 19th century saw something of an international race to distinguish and name other geological systems, recognisable 'packages' of strata, representing discrete periods of prehistoric time. Also, in 1822 d'Omalius d'Halloy named a group of *Flötz-Schichten* or Secondary strata as the *Terrain Cretacé*, which is now universally known as the Cretaceous Period.

In Britain, the lure of geological time 'grabbing' attracted the attentions of a young ex-army officer, Roderick Impey Murchison. Much of the general distribution of strata across England had been mapped out already by William Smith and separately by a consortium of Geological Society of London members, under the leadership of George Bellas Greenough. The relatively simple geological structure of much of these younger strata in England helped the mapping process. However, in south-west England, Wales, the north of England and beyond into Scotland, the rocks are generally older and structurally more complex. Below the *Flötz-Schichten* or Secondary strata lay the Carboniferous and Transition Series that

were known to contain some organic remains and were thought to record the beginnings of life.

Strata of Carboniferous age were worked for coal in Shropshire from the early part of the 18th century, providing the basis of the local iron industry and the foundation of the Industrial Revolution in Britain. Below and to the west lay the older rocks of the Welsh Borders and Wales which became known as Transition, Grauwacke or Graywackes, and were generally undifferentiated or mapped in any detail. Even Smith's 1815 geological map of England and Wales and the slightly more sophisticated 1819 compilation map of Greenough showed these older rocks of Wales, the Lake District, south-west England and most of Scotland as 'terra incognita'. Smith's nephew, John Phillips, wrote that 'before the Summer of 1831 the whole field of the ancient rocks and fossils... was unexplored but then arose two men... Adam Sedgwick and Roderick Murchison and simultaneously set to work to cultivate what had been left a desert'. As usual, the truth is somewhat more complex.

The story that is generally told in books about the history of geological investigation in Britain is that the first systematic investigation of the strata of the Transition, Grauwacke and Primary rocks of Wales was undertaken by Roderick Impey Murchison and Adam Sedgwick in the 1820s and 1830s.

Murchison was of a genteel but relatively poor Scottish background. He had served as an officer in the

RIGHT:

Illustration of Silurian landscapes of the Welsh borderlands originally sketched by Murchison's wife, Charlotte, for his 1839 book The Silurian System

British army in Spain during the Peninsular War but had retired young, upon making a 'good' marriage. Although he was inclined to the usual pursuits of hunting and shooting, his wife encouraged him to do something more useful and so he attended geology lectures in London that sufficiently enthused him to take up the hammer instead of the gun. As a man of independent means he could spend as much time as he wanted in the field, and with his social connections was able to make use of the hospitality of local gentry and aristocracy.

By contrast Adam Sedgwick, son of a Cumbrian vicar and schoolteacher, had done well enough scholastically to gain a sizarship to Cambridge University. This meant that he had partly to pay his way by waiting upon his fellow students; it was a well-trodden route for clever but poor students to gain degrees. Sedgwick did exceptionally well, was elected a fellow of Trinity College in 1810, was ordained at Norwich in 1817, and appointed to the Woodwardian chair of mineralogy in the university and a fellowship of the Geological Society in 1818, despite only having a limited knowledge of geology. He soon made up for this deficiency and was the first Woodwardian professor in many years to take his duties seriously. From 1822–4 Sedgwick made the first systematic geological survey of the Lake District and met Murchison, and together they geologised in Scotland, Devonshire and Wales in the 1830s. Sedgwick's time in the field was limited to the university vacations, and even then he had ecclesiastical duties in Norwich to attend to.

In Wales, the two friends decided to see if they could make geological sense of the unknown terrain of the Grauwacke Series. Sedgwick, by this time the more experienced geologist of the two and used to working in folded and faulted strata, started his mapping from the oldest, Primary rocks of North Wales with the intention of mapping his way south and east. Murchison was to work his way down from a known base line in younger rocks. Before starting out he assiduously 'picked the brains' of any geological acquaintances who knew anything about the Grauwacke strata. As a result he started his investigation from the southern end of the Wye Valley and worked his way down the stratigraphic succession from the Old Red Sandstone strata into progressively older rocks, noting their characteristics and fossil content as he went.

In retrospect, Murchison claimed that his mapping in Wales followed 'Smithian' stratigraphic principles, and he certainly took care to characterise his rock units by listing their fossil contents. Although he did acknowledge some of the help he received, he was sparing in his admission of just how much groundwork had already been laid down by a number of investigators in the region. In the introduction to *The Silurian System*, the book he wrote in 1839 synthesising his work in Wales, Murchison stated that 'having discovered that the region formerly inhabited by the Silures... contained a vast and regular succession of undescribed deposits of a remote age [I had] named them'. He went on to say that 'no one was aware of the existence below the Old Red Sandstone of a regular series of deposits containing peculiar organic remains' which was seriously economical with the truth. William Fitton (1780–1861), Arthur Aitkin (1773–1854) and Rev T.T. Lewis (1801–58) were just some of the people who had made serious investigations of parts of the local geology. There were many others, stretching back decades, such as the German mineralogist Rudolf Erich Rapse (1737–94), better known as the author of the fantastical *Singular Travels, Campaigns and Adventures of Baron Munchausen*, who discovered lead ores near Shrewsbury in the 1780s.

As historians of geology such as Hugh Torrens have recently pointed out, there is a serious discrepancy between our knowledge of the history of practical geology in Britain and the development of its more academic theories. Considering that the Industrial Revolution began well within the latter part of the 18th century, and that it was so dependent on geological materials, how is it possible that it should have succeeded so spectacularly in Britain when it was apparently in advance of the theorising? There must have been a considerable body of knowledge within practitioners operating outside the gentlemanly cliques of the metropolis and the few universities that 'indulged' in science.

The Rev Lewis was particularly important for Murchison since he 'had the honour of conducting Mr Murchison... along the path of an old road... presenting a continuous section from the lower Ludlow rock to the Old Red Sandstone... in his first visit to Herefordshire [in] July 1831'. The succession of Ludlow strata and those immediately below had been worked out by Arthur Aikin before 1812 during an attempt to survey the region geologically, an attempt that failed through lack of money. Murchison saw Aikin's notes and drawings, and was still repeating Aikin's confusion of the Wenlock and Aymestry Limestones as late as 1833.

The geological situation that confronted Sedgwick was much more complex. Not only are the strata of North Wales difficult to subdivide because so many of them look similar in the field and generally lack fossil content, but they are often highly deformed by folds and displaced by faults. Sedgwick struggled to make sense of the order of the

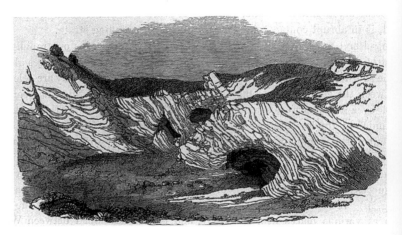

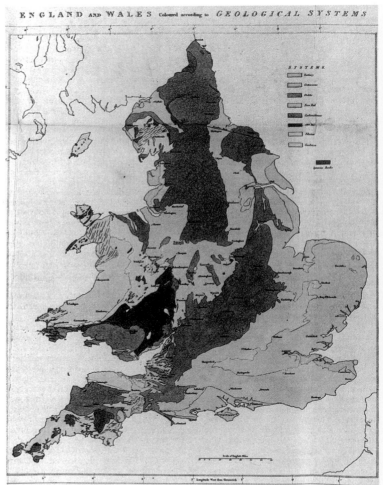

ENGLAND AND WALES Coloured according to GEOLOGICAL SYSTEMS

strata, and even when he did find fossils was not so assiduous as Murchison in identifying them. Nevertheless, by 1835 both geologists were convinced that they had each recognised distinct new systems of strata that should replace the old Transition name. Sedgwick named his the Cambrian (after the Roman name for Wales – *Cambria*) and distinguished it as a series of strata lying above the Primary rocks of

ABOVE:
The geological map of England and Wales published by Murchison in The Silurian System *with the Cambrian reduced to a small region of north Wales*

Anglesey and below Murchison's Silurian System, which was named after the Silures, a Romano-Celtic hill tribe. At first they were happy that the mutual boundary between the two systems was geologically secure, but it did not stay that way for long. Sedgwick's initial failure to list his Cambrian fossil fauna allowed the subsequent conflict over the definition of the boundary between the Cambrian and Silurian to escalate.

Murchison was no palaeontologist but he recruited a number of experts – such as

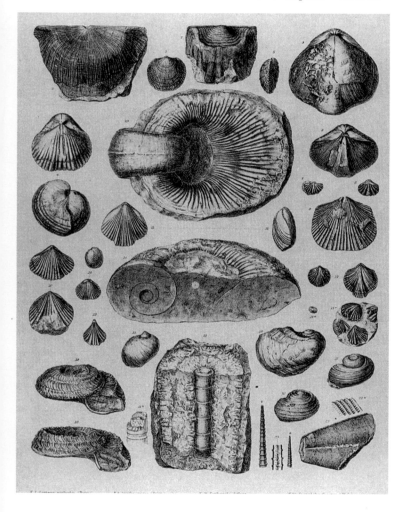

J. de C. Sowerby who had general expertise in identifying invertebrate fossils; J.L.R. Agassiz, the Swiss glaciologist and expert on fossil fish; and W. Lonsdale, who specialised in the identification of fossil corals – to help illustrate and describe his Silurian faunas in his famous three-part work of 1839, *The Silurian System*. Over the following decades Murchison elaborated upon 'his' Silurian System and in

1854 published the first edition of *Siluria. A History of the Oldest Fossiliferous Rocks and their Foundations* which, as its title indicates, was not only a synthesis of his many academic publications but also laid claim to the origin of life within the Silurian. The book went into a number of editions over the years and its wide distribution helped promote acceptance of the Silurian System both nationally and internationally. But it was the adoption of the Murchisonian version by the Geological Survey of Great Britain and Ireland which finally painted so much of the Lower Palaeozoic outcrop of these islands the characteristic Silurian blue, a situation that lasted until the early 1900s. It was perhaps no accident that the Survey should adopt Murchison's version since he was director of it from 1855.

From the 1840s the development of the conflict between Sedgwick and Murchison over the definition of the boundary between the Cambrian and Silurian, resulted in Murchison extending the base of the Silurian downwards. This allowed Murchison to claim that the very origin of life, as represented by the oldest organic remains, was to be found within an enlarged Silurian. If this was true, it had a very far-reaching implication for Sedgwick's Cambrian because it excluded the possibility that Sedgwick would be able to define the Cambrian on the basis of its contained fossils. By Murchison's definition any fossils that were found were Silurian, and therefore the rocks that contained them were also Silurian. Murchison seemed to be supported by evidence from Bohemia, where the French geologist Joachim Barrande (1799–1883) established a sequence of 'étages' (stages 'a' to 'g') within the Silurian. Etage 'c' contained what Barrande called the 'First' or 'Primordial Fauna', below which were the even older unfossiliferous rocks. Some members of this limited fauna of Etage 'c' were in fact genera that British Geological Survey palaeontologist J.W. Salter found in North Wales in 1854. Murchison's claim that the origin of life itself was recorded within 'his' Silurian System was widely accepted. It was portrayed in one of the very first attempts to chronicle the history of life pictorially, published in an English broadsheet *The*

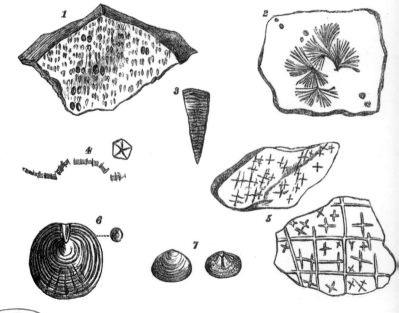

Antediluvian World. By 1858 this view was even more widely distributed by its depiction in the second edition of a popular book on the *Primitive World in Its Different Periods of Formation* by the Austrian botanist, Franz Xavier Unger (1800–70). However, by the 1860s it had become clear to many geologists that there was a distinct Cambrian fauna to be found below the Silurian and that therefore life had originated much earlier than Murchison claimed.

During the late 1840s and 1850s fossils from Barrande's Primordial fauna had been found in Scandinavia and North America, and their distinctiveness from the Silurian fauna gradually became more apparent. Furthermore there was emerging evidence of primitive life, such as the trace fossil *Oldhamia* from Ireland, having existed in the older rocks. Murchison eventually conceded in the second edition of *Siluria* (1859) that such ill-defined fossils might be Cambrian in age but still adhered to a Silurian age for well-defined and stratigraphically useful shelly invertebrates, such as trilobites and brachiopods.

The problems of definition of the Cambro-Silurian boundary took a long time to resolve. Although Charles Lapworth (1842–1920), the Scottish schoolmaster turned geologist, was able to demonstrate and justify the separation and

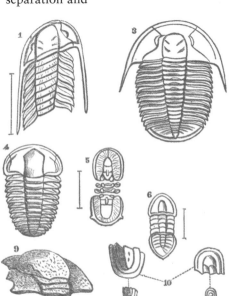

reallocation of much of the Lower Silurian as a major division in its own right in 1879, it was several decades before this new tripartite division of the Lower Palaeozoic was generally accepted. Lapworth had named his new division as the Ordovician System after the Ordovices, another of the Welsh tribes of Roman Britain. From investigations in the Southern Uplands of Scotland, Wales and the Lake District, and using his newly discovered detailed knowledge of the vertical distribution of graptolite fossils, Lapworth was able to subdivide and correlate Lower Palaeozoic strata with a refinement and confidence that had previously been unobtainable. Detailed biozonation of this kind had been developed first in the 1850s by the German palaeontologist Oppel (1831–65) within younger strata of the Jurassic using ammonites.

Lapworth's breakthrough in the development of biozonation marked the beginning of the modern phase of Lower Palaeozoic biostratigraphy and the redefinition of the Silurian System. Despite repeated efforts of successive International

ABOVE:
By the latter part of the 19th century fossils typical of Sedgwick's Cambrian System were known to include worm burrows (1), sponges (5), brachiopods (6–7) and Oldhamia (2)

LEFT:
Fossils that were to prove most useful in subdividing the Cambrian period were the trilobites, part of a great diversity of arthropods that had evolved by this time

Geological Congresses from 1878 onwards to standardise global stratigraphic nomenclature and its usage, it was not until the late 1950s and 1960s that the movement finally succeeded in relation to the Lower Palaeozoic systems.

Fossil remains from the British Silurian have helped reveal important aspects of evolution, such as the distinctiveness of the Palaeozoic biota, the early evolution of fish, the first land-living animals and vascular plants, the application and development of the concept of marine seabed communities within the Silurian and their evolution within the Lower Palaeozoic.

The details of fossil taxonomy and the temporal arrangement of their species within successive strata occupied many geologists throughout the 19th and 20th centuries as they struggled to map and correlate between deposits of similar age around the world. The situation is complicated by the fact that the deposits

and their contained fossils change laterally in response to environmental changes such as water depth and climate. Making connections between contemporary deposits on land and at the bottom of the sea can be particularly difficult as they have no original organisms in common. Correlation depends mainly on some land-derived fossils, especially plant material such as pollen being carried into offshore deposits by water and wind currents.

Public interest in fossils was, however, to be stimulated by a number of different discoveries stretching back to the beginning of the 19th century. Again it was mostly a question of the identification of the large bones of some land-living animals – but not those of elephant relatives. This time the monsters were not readily recognisable for they belonged to a completely unexpected group of extinct reptiles that eventually became known as dinosaurs.

BELOW:
Typical Silurian fossils including brachiopods, a starfish, seasnail and trilobites

Chapter 5

Birds, dinosaurs and evolution

Pliny Moody and the big birds

In 1802 a Massachusetts boy by the name of Pliny Moody found some strange fossils whilst ploughing on his father's farm at South Hadley. His ploughshare turned up a slab of rock on which there were five small but clear footprints. It made enough of an impression upon the young Moody for him to take the rock home. The slab ornamented their farmhouse doorway for at least seven years until Pliny went away to college. According to the story subsequently told by Edward Hitchcock (1793–1864), the Massachusetts State geologist and professor at Amherst College, the slab was then purchased by a Dr Elihu Dwight, who was equally intrigued by the footprints. According to Hitchcock, 'Dr Dwight used pleasantly to remark to his visitors, that these were probably the tracks of Noah's raven'.

Some 30 years later, in 1839, Professor Hitchcock (who made a particular study of such fossil footprints) acquired the slab for his collection. In 1841 he described them as *Ornithoidichnites fulicoides*, meaning 'bird-like footprints similar to the coot' because they resembled the footprints of the American coot *Fulica americana*.

Hitchcock's interest in fossil footprints had been stimulated by a local physician, Dr James Deane. In 1835 Deane heard about some unusual stone slabs from a local quarry that were to be laid as a sidewalk in Greenfield, Massachusetts. The

slabs were, according to a local man, Mr W.W. Draper, covered in 'turkey tracks made 3,000 years ago'. Deane wrote to Hitchcock about the discovery and persuaded him to come and look at them for himself. Excited by the novelty of the discovery, Hitchcock searched local quarries which contained the same kind of red sandstones and found more examples. He compared the fossil footprints with those of living animals and published his conclusions in 1836. The Connecticut Valley fossil footprints with their three toes were, according to Hitchcock, made by antediluvian birds. He called them *Ornithoidichnites*, whilst by comparison tracks made by reptiles were *Sauroidichnites* and four-footed tracks were *Tetrapodichnites*.

Over the following years Hitchcock elaborated his classification by combining these 'ichnogenus' names with those of 'ichnospecies' to produce ichnotaxa that accorded with general taxonomic practice. This procedure has been used with such fossil footprints and other trace fossils ever since. Rarely is it ever known what exact fossil species made any particular trackway because organisms that make tracks do not generally drop dead in them and leave an identifiable body fossil. So there is a parallel nomenclature of body fossil taxa and ichnotaxa, some of which must be synonymous.

Hitchcock's enthusiasm for fossil footprints grew. In many ways he was one of the founding 'fathers' of what he called

OPPOSITE:
In 1802 Pliny Moody, a Massachusetts farm boy, dug up a rock slab covered with footprints which eventually passed into the hands of a Dr Dwight, who regarded them as footprints made by Noah's raven

RIGHT:
Hitchcock's collection of fossil footprints was so large that a museum specifically for it was built at Amherst College

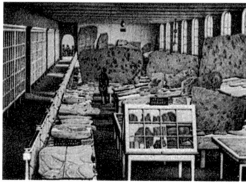

'ichnolithology', meaning 'the study of footprints in stone'. Today the subject is known more succinctly as ichnology. Hitchcock's collection of track-bearing rock slabs eventually took up the whole ground floor of a specially built museum – the Appleton Cabinet – at Amherst College. Meanwhile Deane, who was also interested in fossil tracks, was annoyed that Hitchcock had claimed priority for the discovery. Hitchcock defended himself by arguing that nobody in the scientific world would have known about them if he had not published their details. The row rumbled on acrimoniously for years.

A poem (of sorts) by Hitchcock, posthumously published by his son, gives some insight into the attitude towards fossils that still prevailed in the mid-19th century amongst more conservative geologists.

The Sandstone Bird
by Edward Hitchcock

Scene: Banks of the Connecticut River; geologist alone examining the footmarks of a bird (*Ornithichnites giganteus*)

Foot-marks on stone! how plain and
*   yet how strange!*
A bird track truly though of giant
*   bulk,*
Yet of the monster every vestige else
Has vanished. Bird, a problem thou
*   hast solved*
Man never has: to leave his trace on
*   earth*
Too deep for time and fate to wear
*   away.*
A thousand pyramids had mouldered
*   down*
Since on this rock thy footprints were
*   impressed;*
Yet here it stands unaltered though
*   since then,*
Earth's crust has been upheaved and
*   fractured oft.*
And deluge after deluge o'er her
*   driven,*
Has swept organic life from off her
*   face.*
Bird of a former world, would that
*   thy form*

Might reappear in these thy ancient
*   haunts...*
Pre-adamic bird, whose sway
Ruled creation in thy day,
Come obedient to my word,
Stand before Creation's Lord...

Hitchcock also celebrated his vision of the past world of the Connecticut Valley in prose. In 1848 he proclaimed that, 'I have experienced all the excitement of romance, as I have gone back into those immensely remote ages, and watched those shores along which these enormous and heteroclitic beings walked. Now I have seen, in scientific vision, an apterous bird, some twelve or fifteen feet high – nay large flocks of them – walking over the muddy surface, followed by many others of analogous character, but of smaller size. Next comes a bipedal animal, a bird perhaps, with a foot and heel nearly two feet long... Strange, indeed, this menagerie of remote sandstone days'.

At the time, Hitchcock's interpretation was perfectly sound and reasonable, scientifically. The only animals known to produce such bipedal trackways made up of three-toed footprints were birds. The main problem was that there were no living birds that reached anything like 4 or 5m (12 or 15ft) in height. However, in 1838 Hitchcock's

bird theory got a considerable lift.

The British anatomist Richard Owen, using the same methods of comparative anatomy employed so effectively by Cuvier a generation before, described a single short fragment, some 15cm (6in) long, of a thigh bone from New Zealand. He predicted it had belonged to a giant flightless bird known to the Maori people as a moa. Five years later his startling speculation was vindicated when he received a nearly complete specimen, which he called *Dinornis*, meaning 'terrible/awe-inspiring bird'. It stood 3.5m (12ft) tall and had tridactyle (three-toed) feet.

The only problem was that *Dinornis* and the other extinct moas were far too recent to have had anything to do with the Connecticut Valley tracks, which are of late Triassic and early Jurassic age and around 200 million years old. The moas were part of the so-called megafauna of Quaternary 'Ice Age' times and had become extinct along with so many of them, such as the mammoth, sabre-tooth cats and the giant marsupials of Australasia, through human intervention. Nevertheless, Owen had shown that such large birds lived in the past and so it appeared that there was no great reason why they should not have existed in even more remote times.

Meanwhile, as we shall see, back in Europe other important fossil discoveries were being made which were to revolutionise our view of the past and in

particular the interpretation of Hitchcock's footprints. In addition there was a gathering storm brewing over questions of the history of life and its development through time, otherwise known as evolution. Again, Richard Owen was one of the key players in the drama.

Creation – the revised version

In 1844 a book called the *Vestiges of the Natural History of Creation* was published in London. It was a hugely ambitious synthesis that appeared at just the right moment in Victorian intellectual and cultural development. Hell was in decline and the appeal of a vengeful God was wearing off. There was a thirst for knowledge that was increasingly being slaked by the 'industrialisation of print culture', as Cambridge historian of science James Secord calls it. Like Frankenstein, *Vestiges* was a curious hybrid, combining lots of ''ologies'' – from anthropology, through geology and psychology to theology – with the odd ''onomy'' – such as astronomy – thrown in for good measure. Furthermore there was a wonderfully alluring, gossipy mystery to its authorship, because it was anonymous.

Vestiges suggested that life could be created in the laboratory and that humans had evolved from apes, and as such was potentially heretical to many religiously minded people of the time. No one seemed to know who the author was, or anything about his/her social status, politics or gender; but speculation about its authorship kept its sales going for years. Byron's daughter Ada Lovelace was one possibility; Thackeray another; then there were the three scientific Charles's – Babbage, Lyell and Darwin – and so on. By the 1880s some syntactical clues were pointing to an author from north of Hadrian's Wall, and in 1884, 40 years after publication, it was finally confirmed that Robert Chambers (1802–71), the Edinburgh writer and publisher of popular encyclopedias, biographies and reference books, was the author. Chambers never had to face his critics since he died in 1871.

Vestiges hit just the right note and attracted readers from 'toffs' to handloom weavers, including Queen Victoria, Tennyson, Florence Nightingale, Gladstone, Disraeli, Darwin and some 40,000 others in Britain alone. The Whig aristocrat, Lord Morpeth, thought that the progressive development argued for in the book did not 'conflict more with the Mosaic accounts than the received theories of modern Geology; the order assigned to the appearance of man certainly harmonises with them'. Nevertheless, he did dislike the book's views on human origins, as he admitted. 'I do not much care for the notion that we are engendered by monkeys.' Secord, who has written a wonderful comprehensive book on *Vestiges* as a cultural phenomenon, claims that it appealed to progressive Whig aristocracy because it was 'visionary, daring, unfettered by prejudice'.

Tennyson noted that it 'seems to contain many speculations with which I have been familiar for years...' and that there was 'nothing degrading in the theory...' according to which God worked through a law that brought forth new species and that Man's spiritual sense and reason were the products of development. But others saw it as a 'dangerous serpent' which was 'poisoning the spiritual mind of the nation', especially the increasing class of female philosophers who were led by its 'most honied sweetness, to the most tasteful, and to the bitterest fruit'. Bound in scarlet cloth, the book was like the 'whore of Babylon'.

The *North British Review* commented in

August 1845 that, 'If it has been revealed to man that the Almighty made him out of the dust of the earth, and breathed into his nostrils the breath of life, it is in vain to tell a Christian that man was originally a speck of albumen, and passed through stages of monads and monkeys, before he attained his intellectual pre-eminence. If it be a received truth that the Creator has repeatedly interposed in the government of the universe, and displayed his immediate agency in miraculous interpositions, it is an insult to any reader to tell him that being slumbers on his throne, and rules under a "primal arrangement in his counsels", and "by a code of laws of unbending operation".'

In 1849 the Scots geologist and journalist Hugh Miller (1802–56) published

ABOVE:
Not until after his death was the Edinburgh publisher Robert Chambers revealed as the author of the bestselling Vestiges of the Natural History of Creation

OPPOSITE:
Some of the fossil fish and other fossils of the Devonian age Old Red Sandstone, many of which Miller found in the far north of Scotland

Stonemason, ardent protestant and naturalist Hugh Miller firmly believed that the testimony of the rocks would reveal his God's truth. He shot himself dead in 1856

Miller claimed in 1847 that the bony head shield of this early fossil fish was so complex that it argued against the evolutionary story that primitive fish were simple

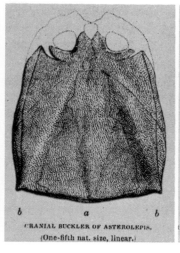

CRANIAL BUCKLER OF ASTEROLEPIS.
(One-fifth nat. size, linear.)

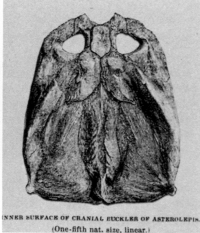

INNER SURFACE OF CRANIAL BUCKLER OF ASTEROLEPIS.
(One-fifth nat. size, linear.)

Foot-prints of the Creator, a book-length attack on *Vestiges*. His main line of attack was against the notion of progression of life. Miller used his own discoveries of some bizarre fossil armoured fish that he argued were very complex and yet were found in very ancient Old Red Sandstone strata in the Orkney Isles. Above all, Miller argued that the last days of human history would not be an advance on the present, but would represent the millennial transformation, the final triumph of Christ over sin and death. The possibility of salvation set man apart from the mere animal vitality of the brutes. If transmutation were true, there was no reason that we should not be 'by nature *atheists*, like dogs'.

With such splendidly polarised credentials *Vestiges* was the 'biggest literary phenomenon for decades', outselling some of Dickens's early novels. These days *Vestiges* tends to be written off as a failed precursor to Darwin's *The Origin of Species*, published 15 years later in 1859, but by the end of the century *Vestiges* had sold just as many copies. The big difference was that although *Vestiges* included some serious mistakes of fact and interpretation, it was a book about evolution for the

people, whereas *The Origin* was a scientific tract which attempted to dot all the 'i's' and cross all the 't's', and was primarily written by Darwin with his scientific peers and critics in mind. Unwittingly Chambers did Darwin a considerable service, partly by drawing the fire of the anti-evolutionists and by warning him of the level of criticism to expect, the directions the lines of fire were likely to take and their points of origin.

Considering that the fossil record contains much of what we know of the history of life, it is perhaps surprising that in *The Origin of Species* Darwin says remarkably little about fossils but does explain at length why he is not doing so. He had learned more than enough from former mentors such as Adam Sedgwick, Woodwardian professor of geology in the University of Cambridge, and from hearing current debates about fossils at the Geological Society in London, to know that the fossil record was a quagmire of problematic information and that many palaeontologists were deeply opposed to the idea of evolution. Foremost amongst these were Adam Sedgwick and Richard Owen, both of whom had written lengthy attacks on *Vestiges*. Both were extremely well informed about the fossil record, much more so than Darwin, both were strong-willed and could be outspoken and powerful enemies.

Owen in particular was a dangerous opponent because of his deep knowledge of biology and anatomy, and he could be positively venomous in his attack both verbally and via the written word. He was deeply ambitious and would do almost anything to make his way in the intensely competitive social and professional marketplace of mid-Victorian England. He saw that there were two main lines of attack open to him. One was the question, also raised by Hugh Miller, of whether there had been progress and improvement in life with adaptation throughout geological history as the evolutionists claimed. The other was the question of whether the fossil record contained evidence for transitional forms between the major groups of life, as it should do if these groups shared common ancestors as the theory claimed.

Darwin was only too well aware of these problems. He spelled them out as raising major objections to his theory and devoted a whole chapter of *The Origin of Species* to explaining why the imperfections of the fossil record were so great that it could not provide the relevant information. His line was that only certain types of organisms are preserved as fossils, mainly the shells of sea-dwelling invertebrates such as molluscs, echinoderms, arthropods and so on that were deposited in ancient marine sediments. Furthermore there was evidence that there were many gaps between the piles of predominantly marine sediment that had been accreted into land masses as the then known sequences of rock strata. Consequently he argued that the record was so biased and fragmentary that it was not surprising that linking forms were not found, and that we should not expect to find them.

Owen, however, saw that new discoveries of peculiarly large fossil bones of extinct reptiles might provide a very good example of successful organisms that clearly had existed in the past but no longer did so. If this were to be true, where would the idea of progress through evolution and survival of the fittest stand? Owen opened a veritable Pandora's box when he coined a name for this extinct group of reptiles, for he called them dinosaurs.

LEFT:
At the height of his success Richard Owen tutored some of Queen Victoria's children and had the 'ear' of Prince Albert, which doubtless helped promote the scheme for a fossil 'theme park' at Sydenham

The dinosaurs – a great British invention

Before 1842 dinosaurs did not exist because they had not been 'invented'. Some puzzling reptile fossils had been found scattered through Jurassic and Cretaceous strata in the south of England but there was no category of dinosaur to place them in. The taxonomic class Dinosauria was invented by the British anatomist Richard Owen to accommodate these petrified remains, many of which seemed to belong to some very large animals.

By the early decades of the 19th century the megafauna of the world's lands and seas was well known, and the chances of any very large animals remaining hidden in remote forests or even in the depths of the oceans was remote. These fossil giants were clearly extinct. Before this time, neither 19th-century England nor the rest of the world had any notion that there had ever been such animals; dinosaurs were not mentioned in the Bible nor any of the earlier accounts of the ancient world. The unfolding history of the Earth did not match the Mosaic version, but curiously many of the scientists promoting the revolution in palaeontology were still vehement believers in the Creation story, even if it was not exactly the version presented in the Old Testament.

The idea that Earth had once been occupied by a previously unknown group of reptiles was remarkable enough; but the revelation that such complex and advanced fossil reptiles had dominated the Earth and then disappeared long before humans existed was totally unexpected. To Richard Owen, author of the name 'dinosaur', their existence seemed to argue against any notion of a prehistoric 'progression' in life.

Although dinosaur remains were first found in Britain and the name coined by a British anatomist, it was not long before the vastly greater geological resources of the New World of the Americas began to extend the potential of the dinosaur as an icon to replace that of the dragons of legend and folklore.

Unfortunately for British dinophiles, the Jurassic and Cretaceous strata of southern Britain are mostly shallow marine deposits, which is why fossils of land-living dinosaurs are not common in them. By comparison the much greater thicknesses of Mesozoic-age terrestrial sedimentary strata of parts of North America, Mongolia and South America are relatively rich in the fossils of dinosaurs and other land-living animals. The existence of any British dinosaur fossils at all is largely due to the fact that there was an archipelago of islands scattered through the shallow seas which separated North America from Britain, Europe and Asia (Eurasia). Sea-level changes allowed the migration of dinosaurs across these 'stepping stones', and occasionally their remains were washed into coastal deposits.

However, it was the abundant new finds and evidence from the New World that questioned the old Imperial model of what a dinosaur looked like. Just as Darwin's theory of evolution was hijacked as a battle-cry for free enterprise, so the image of the dinosaur was lifted from the abysmal swamps and promoted. Cleaned up to remove any unhealthy taint of Gothic decadence, the dinosaur was repackaged to fit Tennyson's epithet for Darwinian evolution 'nature, red in tooth and claw'. From crow-sized animals to beasts larger than any other land-living animals ever known, the dinosaurs have continued to fascinate scientists and the wider public ever since.

From the early decades of the 19th century scientists had a fundamental problem with the image of the dinosaurs. They were trying to put together a very difficult jigsaw puzzle. There were very few pieces (bones) of the puzzle left and many of these were broken. Furthermore, they had little idea of what the overall picture should be. The most obvious model was provided by surviving reptiles such as the lizards and crocodiles. But there was one major difference: the size of the fossil bones showed that many of the reptiles of the past were built on a much grander scale. Here was a new image to conjure with. To begin with the concept of the dinosaur was not constrained too much by fact and could be transformed at will.

Nineteenth-century scientists, artists and journalists willingly gave a receptive public a variety of icons they could relate to. For those with a melodramatic tendency, there was an exciting whiff of brimstone and fire about dinosaurs as they were endowed with the mantle of the mythical dragons. For the religious, not only were they potentially dangerous but also sinful by association with the 'lowly creeping serpents' of the Bible. For admirers of the Gothic, they were suffused with the foul stench of the 'abysmal slimy swamps' of antediluvian time. Whilst some of the scientists enjoyed the publicity associated with the more emotional interpretations, others took a more formal and grandiose approach.

In keeping with the growing might of imperial England, it is perhaps no accident that the developing picture of the dinosaurs took on a more dominating image which reflected something much more imposing, more powerful and terrible. Like Victorian England itself, the dinosaurs came to be seen as the ruling class of their day, which held a global hegemony. The irony is that whilst the Victorians were very keen on modelling themselves on such past empire builders – be they dinosaurs, Greeks or Romans – they never seemed to learn that all such dominion eventually goes into terminal 'decline and fall'. Except, that is, for Richard Owen, who thought that the rise and fall of the dinosaurs provided evidence against Darwin's theory of evolution.

Today dinosaurs have expanded into an extraordinary array of beasts ranging from bird-sized and bird-like to vast lumbering behemoths, whose size and strength seems to defy the laws of biology. Now some dinosaur experts claim that there were predatory dinosaurs such as the giant tyrannosaurs that were highly active, warm-blooded killers, who outshone any mammalian carnivores for sheer bulk, ferocity and ability to create mayhem. However, other experts question such portrayals and are producing evidence that limits the speeds at which such large beasts could have moved, and rather sees them as scavengers and at best ambush hunters that avoided taking too many risks.

Being long dead, the dinosaurs have the advantage of never having been observed in action by human beings, so they offer enormous potential for speculative reconstruction. Even so, no matter how fanciful the interpretation, there are still the unalterable facts provided by the fossil record for their existence and size. There is no doubting the 'ooh-aah' factor of the dinosaurs. Some of them really were the largest plant eaters and meat eaters to have ever existed on land.

It is ironic that part of Owen's reason for creating this special category of animals was to try and stem what he thought was the growing danger of the idea that there was evidence for progress in past life. He thought he could stop the growth of such a dangerous heresy by showing that the dinosaurs, as an advanced group of reptiles, had become extinct. Little did Richard Owen realise what he was creating in 1842 when he invented the Dinosauria. Like Dr Frankenstein, he certainly made a monster but, unlike Mary Shelley's scientist, he also generated a whole new realm of fact and fiction, almost unbelievable fossils and a renaissance in animal fantasy. If only Owen had registered copyright of the name dinosaur he would have become monstrously rich.

Today the very word 'dinosaur' has taken on a double meaning. There is the metaphorical 'has been, consigned to the dustbin of history' and then there are the 'terrible lizards' of the first theme park in the world, the rebuilt Crystal Palace in south London and its modern fictional counterpart 'Jurassic Park', both beloved by children of all ages from the 1850s to the present day. These dinosaurs are either portrayed as benign plant eaters, or as the 'bad guys', the red-eyed, ravenous, meat-eating predators. But the image of the dinosaur has gone through a number of transformations in its passage through the last 160 years, since taking over the mantle of the dragon.

From discoveries of jumbled bones to the wonderful finds of complete skeletons in the Badlands of the Midwest of America, the remains of these mysterious animals combine immensity of size with the curiously unexpressive, staring creepiness of reptiles. How much truth is there behind this image – what were these dinosaurs really like? Does their rise and fall justify their status as an object lesson in why not to overdo things and become victims to your own success? Did they fall because they were unable to adapt and change, or were they blasted off the face of the earth by a meteorite? Did it all end with a bang or a whimper?

From late Carboniferous times, over 300

BELOW:
As befitted the times, the image of the extinct dinosaurs had been transformed by Owen and his artist Waterhouse Hawkins from that of lowly creeping serpents into one of imperial might by the mid 19th century

million years before humans appeared on Earth, a group of scaly-skinned, egg-laying reptiles evolved and gradually came to dominate the planet. For over 155 million years these extinct reptiles, which came to be known as dinosaurs, ruled the landscapes of the world from Alaska to Antarctica. No other group of animals has been so successful for so long. The mammals have only been in charge for a mere 65 million years. One of the great mysteries of the dinosaurs is why, if they were so successful, did they die out 65 million years ago? Why should the dinosaurs have been 'deselected', whilst other reptiles like the terrestrial crocodiles and lizards and aquatic turtles survived and prospered? There are more kinds of reptiles alive today (some 6,000 species) than there are kinds of mammals (a mere 4,250 or so, of which nearly a half are rodents).

Discovering dinosaurs

In the early decades of the 19th century the Reverend Doctor William Buckland, Reader in Mineralogy in the University of Oxford, was deeply concerned that the discoveries of the newly emergent science of geology would confirm the basic truths of the order of Creation and the story of the Flood as portrayed in the Old Testament. In his lectures he debated whether the 'days' of the Creation story might in fact correspond to more lengthy creative eras, as the geological data seemed to indicate. A Dickensian figure, Buckland was also famous for his eccentricity: he had a menagerie of sundry pets, ranging from guinea pigs to a jackal (that was occasionally to be heard crunching one of the guinea pigs under the sofa) and a bear, named Tiglath Pileser after the founder of the Assyrian empire. He also liked culinary experiment and claimed that he had tried eating most living things from mice to crocodile. In his later years his eccentric behaviour deteriorated and descended into real madness.

Buckland was also Director of the Ashmolean Museum, which contained a historic collection of petrified remains, including large bones of some unknown animals. These included the 10kg (22lb) knuckle end of a thigh bone which had

been found in the 17th century in a local quarry. This was described in 1677 by the first keeper of the museum, Dr Robert Plot (1640–96), in his *Natural History of Oxfordshire*. Plot's initial diagnosis was that the bone was from an elephant imported into Britain during the Roman invasion. However, when he had the opportunity to compare the specimen directly with that of an elephant thigh bone, he had to admit that it was different and was forced to conclude that the fossil had 'exactly the figure of the lower most part of the Thigh-bone of a Man'.

During the 18th century more puzzling bones, including teeth, were found locally in the so-called Stonesfield 'slate'. This Jurassic limestone was actively quarried because it could be split into thin slabs that were extensively used as roofing 'slates' in the region. The limestone is often quite fossiliferous, and when the quarrymen came across curious shells and bones they put them aside to be sold to collectors. Some of

*The broken lower jaw
of Buckland's giant
reptile from Stonesfield
in Oxfordshire has the
bladed and serrated
teeth of a predatory
carnivore*

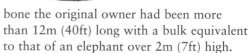

these ended up in the museum.

Cuvier visited the Ashmolean in 1818 to see the collections. From his examination of these problematic bones he concluded that they were more likely to be reptilian than mammalian. One of the fossils was a 30cm (12in) jawbone still armed with impressively long (15cm/6in) backward-curved teeth and other smaller ones as yet unerrupted within the jawbone. Cuvier recognised this as a typically reptilian mode of continuous tooth replacement, but could not be sure what kind of reptile the jaw belonged to. The most obvious comparison was with a crocodile, but the fossil teeth were flattened and quite blade-like with serrated edges, whilst crocodile teeth are more conical and not serrated but sometimes ridged. Cuvier calculated that from the size of the thigh

bone the original owner had been more than 12m (40ft) long with a bulk equivalent to that of an elephant over 2m (7ft) high.

Although Buckland was alerted to this diagnosis by Cuvier in 1818 he did not rush to publish it (perhaps because it hardly fitted into the Biblical scheme of things which he wanted to promote). He published it six years later, mainly because there were then reports of some new giant bones being found in Sussex which were, he heard, being studied by a Dr Gideon Mantell (1790–1852). So on 24 February 1824 Buckland took the opportunity to describe 'his' giant reptile at a meeting of the Geological Society in London, of which he was president at the time. He described the fragmentary Oxfordshire remains and explained how, from the teeth alone, the remains could be assigned to the lizard 'Order Sauria', within the 'Class Reptilia'.

Since the bones had been found associated with the fossils of sea creatures, including crocodile and turtle remains, Buckland concluded that this extinct lizard 'was probably an amphibious animal' but could probably emerge to creep about on the land. The image he created was that of a very big but 'lowly, creeping serpent-like animal' and gave it the name *Megalosaurus* meaning 'great lizard'. In the audience sat Gideon Mantell, whom Buckland had just trumped in the publicity stakes; but Mantell was about to gazump Buckland in the race to describe the biggest beast.

As an apprentice physician, Mantell had the luck to be introduced to Dr James Parkinson (1755–1824), the famous medic and radical reformer who called for universal suffrage to avert bloody social revolution and who described the degenerative condition which still bears his name. Parkinson was an established author

*Dr Gideon Mantell was
a successful physician,
but his obsession with
making a name for
himself as a geologist
ruined both his medical
practice and his
marriage*

of geological books and one of the founder members of the Geological Society of London. In 1811 he published the final volume of his five-volume work *Organic Remains of a Former World* in which he described the distribution of fossils within their original strata. Not surprisingly at this date, he still concluded that the Mosaic account 'is confirmed in every respect, except as to the age of the world, and the distance of time between the completion of different parts of creation' and that overall the creation of the Earth 'must have been the work of a vast length of time'. Parkinson encouraged the young Mantell to pursue his interests in geology.

Following his London medical apprenticeship, Mantell qualified as a physician and returned to Lewes in Sussex where he had grown up. By 1819 he was a well-established and successful medical practitioner, married with a child and actively pursuing his geological interests in the region. From his network of local contacts, gifts of stones and fossils flooded into his house so that it became as much a museum as a home. News of his collection brought well-connected visitors who in turn spread the word amongst the scientific élite. In June 1820 Mantell was sent some fossils that had been unearthed in quarries around the nearby town of Cuckfield. They included fossil backbones, a fragment of a very large leg bone and some teeth. Excited by the finds, he visited the quarries and had the luck to find more pieces of large bones and the metre-long fragment of a fossil tree trunk covered with diamond-shaped scars like tropical palms. His initial thoughts were that the fragmentary remains belonged

to one of the newly discovered sea monsters, marine reptiles such as the ichthyosaurs, but he soon moved towards crocodile affinities and recognised that the fossil tree trunk indicated that land could not have been far away when the deposits were originally laid down.

In the early 1820s another piece of fossil tooth of unusual appearance was found by either Mantell or his wife (the popular story is that it was his wife). With a distinct wear surface on the crown, giving it a blunt end, the tooth was clearly not that of a crocodile but more like that of a mammalian plant eater. The problem was that at the time Mantell knew of no mammal fossils being found in such ancient rock strata, nor of any reptile that masticated its food to produce such a wear surface.

Amongst the bones he had amassed was

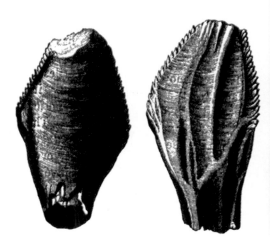

BELOW RIGHT:
Back and front views of one of the strange leaf-shaped and serrated teeth which Mantell puzzled over in the 1820s

BELOW:
The Whiteman's Green stone quarry in the south of England from which Mantell (seated in the foreground) recovered some of his giant reptile bones and teeth

the broken section of a thigh bone measuring 60cm (25in) in circumference. Mantell understood the logic behind the comparative anatomy practised by Cuvier and the contemporary talk of scaling up from measures on individual bones to assess the overall size of an extinct animal. Mantell came up with an animal having the bulk of an elephant and an astonishing length of over 10m (30ft), far bigger than any other fossil creature known at the time.

By 1821 Mantell had heard of the Stonesfield fossils in the Ashmolean and of Buckland's growing interest in them, perhaps from Charles Lyell who had recently visited Mantell to see his collection. The following year, 1822, saw the publication of Mantell's book *Fossils of the South Downs*, the results of his investigations into the geology of Sussex, with illustrations of strata and fossils engraved by his wife. Included was reference to 'the teeth, ribs, and vertebrae of a gigantic animal of the Lizard tribe'.

those of senior members of the society. Lyell even took one of Mantell's fossil teeth to Paris to get Cuvier's opinion, only for the great anatomist to dismiss it as that of a rhinoceros. Although later Cuvier had second thoughts, only his singularly unenthusiastic initial reaction got back to Mantell, much to the latter's disappointment and dismay. After all his hard work, which not only took up his time but also meant neglecting his medical practice and his family, his hopes of rising in the scientific world seemed to be dashed.

When Mantell heard that Buckland was due to lecture on the Stonesfield fossils at the Geological Society, he determined to be there. His intervention in the discussion alerted Buckland to the potential competition coming from the Sussex finds, and Buckland tried to steal Mantell's thunder by incorporating discussion of the Sussex bones and an illustration of them in his own paper. Luckily for Mantell the society's publication committee stopped

BELOW:
The lower jaw and teeth of a modern, plant-eating iguana illustrated by Mantell and compared with his fossil teeth. The iguana had only just been discovered, and Mantell was lucky to have been shown a pickled specimen

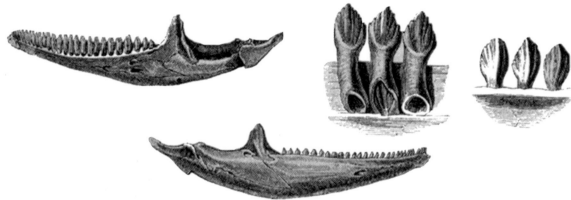

His hope that this book would gain him entré into the select world of the Geological Society were not fulfilled. When he took the fossil teeth to a meeting of the society, the general opinion of the 'experts' was that they belonged to some large fish or a more recent mammal from the diluvium. Sales of the book were another disappointment; they did not nearly cover the cost of publication and Mantell was left with a bill for £300.

Nevertheless, with Lyell's help, in 1823 Mantell managed to get a paper containing his ideas on the Tilgate Forest strata read at a meeting of the Geological Society. Its publication was held up for three years, perhaps because his ideas clashed with

their president from going too far in the interests of fair play. Even so, Buckland does mention that Mantell's Sussex giant must have been twice the size of the Oxford one and pumped the 'reptile from Cuckfield' up to betweeen 'sixty to seventy feet'; but he did not agree that it was a plant eater.

Mantell determined to try his luck again with Cuvier, sending him tooth specimens and drawings of the other fossils. This time Cuvier acknowledged their curious form and at last concluded that Mantell might have a new herbivorous reptile on his hands. Encouraged at last, Mantell visited the Hunterian Museum in London to see if he could find anything resembling his fossil specimens. He found nothing, but luckily a well-informed assistant curator, Samuel Stutchbury, saw that the fossil teeth possessed a passing semblance to those of living iguana, since he was familiar with specimens from the West Indies and had just bottled one from Barbados.

It was just the breakthrough Mantell needed. The iguana's strange leaf-shaped teeth with serrations along the edges and wear surfaces are an adaptation to its plant-eating habits. The only major difference was in the size; the fossils were some 20 times bigger than those of the living beast, which was only a metre long. Mantell quickly did the sums and concluded that 'his' beast must have been more than 20m (over 60ft) long. He proposed that it be called *Iguana-saurus* but was advised by the Reverend William Conybeare, an expert on fossils with a classical education, that *Iguanoides*, meaning 'like an iguana' or, *Iguanodon*, meaning 'iguana tooth', would be better. Mantell chose the latter, and so the beast has been named ever since. Cuvier's mention of Mantell and his curious new beast in a new edition of one of his books on fossils ensured that Mantell's 'star' was at last ascending in the scientific galaxy.

In 1825 his description of *Iguanodon* was read at a meeting of the prestigious Royal Society and later that year the 35-year-old Mantell was elected a Fellow, thus giving him an equivalent scientific status to the members of the Geological Society who had been so chary about recognising his work. But it was nearly 10 years before Mantell had any really significant new material with which to flesh out his *Iguanodon*. The basic problem was that fossils of such beasts, now known to be

land-living dinosaurs, are uncommon within the predominantly marine strata of the south of England. If the region had had the same geology as Dakota or Manitoba in North America or the Brown Hills of Mongolia, there would be plenty of terrestrial strata full of fossils of land-living animals and plants; but then the whole story would have been different.

In May 1834 Mr Bensted, a Kent quarry owner, wrote to Mantell telling him of a new find of giant bones which had been unearthed by his workers in a stone quarry near Maidstone. Mantell's luck was in again; the rock slab included some of the peculiar leaf-shaped *Iguanodon* teeth and a jumble of other bones belonging to the animal that he had not seen before. Mantell's first problem was the fact that Bensted, being a businessman, had realised the potential monetary value of the find and was determined to get as much as he could for it. Only through the intervention of some wealthy friends, who bought the specimen and presented it to him, was

ABOVE:

The so-called 'Mantell-piece', found in 1834 and containing jumbled bones of an Iguanodon, *whose preparation Mantell laboured over*

Mantell able to work on the new slab. He spent long hours laboriously chipping the hard rock matrix away from around the petrified bones whilst trying not to damage them. He made quite a good job of it, considering the fractured nature of many of the bones. For the first time he had part of an actual single skeleton with backbones, ribs, part of the pelvis, foot bones and a single conical spike or horn-shaped bone about 15cm (6in) long.

Again Mantell tried scaling up measures from the bones and found that the beast was getting bigger and bigger. Its shoulder blade measured some 75cm (30in), 20 times bigger than that of iguana, giving *Iguanodon* an estimated length of 30m (100ft). The Geological Society at last recognised Mantell's endeavours and awarded him its prestigious Wollaston Gold Medal in 1835; the only other recipient had been William Smith.

By this time Mantell and his family were established in fashionable Brighton. His medical practice had been doing well, but as he spent more and more time on his geological studies it began to suffer. Word was that Dr Mantell was more interested in his fossils than his patients and, whether true or not, the damage was done and he had to sell first his stocks and shares, then his practice. Most of his grand, fossil-laden museum of a house was let, and the family had to go into lodgings. Eventually, in 1838, his collections had to be sold. After protracted negotiations they were bought by the British Musem for £4,087, and Mantell moved to Clapham in south London, hoping to set up a new practice. His long-suffering wife left him as did the older children; his son Walter, as a newly qualified doctor, emigrated to New Zealand. Tragically a younger daughter, Hannah, died and Mantell fell into deep despair. He also had a new rival in the study of the giant denizens of the geological past, a young man called Richard Owen. Neither Buckland nor Mantell, the pioneers of the terrestrial saurians, were to take the big prize: Owen beat them both to it.

Owen was one of the new breed of professional palaeontologists and a museum man, employed at the Hunterian Museum in London and later in the British Museum. He was bright and very ambitious, knew all about the Cuvierian method of comparative

BELOW:
The image of the dinosaurs has always been one of beasts locked in mortal combat. Here Iguanodon *and* Megalosaurus *battle it out in Louis Figuier's 1863 reconstruction of Lower Cretaceous times*

anatomy, and may well have seen himself as inheriting the mantle of the great man. Owen took every opportunity to further his career. He greatly benefited from the flood of strange animals that were arriving in the capital from the rapidly expanding British Empire and the ever-extending reach of its explorers.

Some weird water-living, hairy and yet egg-laying animals with beaks arrived from Australia. Owen was able to show that the platypus, as it was called, was not some freak or transitional creature between reptiles and mammals but a primitive mammal with mammary glands. He was appointed professor of comparative anatomy at St Bartholomew's Hospital in 1834, elected to fellowship of the Royal Society and then Hunterian Professor at the Royal College of Surgeons. Owen was well on his way in metropolitan society. When Darwin returned from his voyage on the *Beagle*, he donated some 80 mammals and 400 birds to the Zoological Society who determined that they should go to the Hunterian Professor for study. Owen was also given the task of reporting to the British Association for the Advancement of Science (BAAS) on the current 'state of knowledge of the Fossil Reptiles of Great Britain'.

The German biologist Hermann von Meyer had, in 1832, reviewed the classification of the few extinct saurians known at the time. Buckland's *Megalosaurus* with Mantell's *Iguanodon* and *Hylaeosaurus*, which Mantell had also named as a recognisably different beast, were all grouped as saurians with heavy mammal-like limbs and thus unlike any living reptiles. By 1839, after his move to Clapham, the tragic death of his daughter and his separation from his wife, Mantell was too busy trying to build up his new practice to continue studying 'his' fossils, which now belonged to the British Museum and were more accessible to Owen. Owen had the time and energy and made the best of it.

By August 1841 Owen was ready to make his report to the annual meeting of the BAAS which was held in Plymouth that year. Mantell was not in the audience. In a lengthy and detailed report Owen divided the saurians into four, with the marine

reptiles such as the ichthyosaurs and plesiosaurs as entaliosaurians, following Conybeare; secondly there were the crocodilians; thirdly the flying reptiles; and fourthly, following von Meyer, he characterised the three large extinct genera of *Megalosaurus*, *Iguanodon* and *Hylaeosaurus* as 'very singular and very gigantic species which have now utterly perished' and grouped them as 'lizard-like' lacertians. He did not name them as dinosaurs at this 1841 meeting as is so often misreported, although he was working towards it.

Interestingly and most importantly Owen, following Cuvier, pursued his argument that there were no evident transitions or transformation from one form to another to be seen, and no evidence of progression as some naturalists argued. All the evidence pointed to their creation as separate distinct species, each best fitted to its place and role in life. For Owen, the existence of advanced creatures like these giant saurians before the mammals, which included some very primitive forms such as the platypus, was an important part of the argument against the progressionists. He also made critical comments about attempts by people like Mantell for seeking similarities between ancient and living forms such as *Iguanodon* with the iguana.

Owen's presentation, including his critical comments on Mantell's work, was reported at length in some of the journals of the day, such as the *Literary Gazette*. It is likely that these criticisms restimulated Mantell's interest and proprietorial feelings over 'his' giant saurians, which in turn stoked Owen's competitiveness and determination to win the day. Mantell's response was also published in the *Gazette* and the debate continued. But Mantell was struck by yet another misfortune, a traffic accident, which effectively put him out of the competition. He was thrown from a carriage and injured his back and spinal cord when the horses bolted, a common occurrence in those days.

Owen's study of the limb bones of the so-called lacertians increasingly convinced him of their differences to lizard limbs, which stick out sideways from their bodies and cause them to move by throwing their bodies into serpent-like waves from side to

side. Mantell's reconstruction of *Iguanodon* seems to owe as much to medieval imagery as anything else, with a distinctly dragon-like beast, legs sticking out on either side and a long whip-like tail. He placed the spike, rhinoceros-like, on the end of its nose. By contrast, Owen saw that the much larger and heavier extinct forms required their limbs to be brought in under the mass of the body bulk, more like mammals.

The idea that they were lowly creeping beasts (as portrayed by Mantell and Buckland) was about to be overthrown. But in addition Owen realised that the crude scaling exercises of Buckland and Mantell were also rather wild overestimates. So instead he used estimates based on the size of the backbones and recalculated, shrinking the length of *Iguanodon* down to a 3ft (1m) head, 12ft (3.5m) body and 13ft (4m) tail, totalling a mere 28ft (8.5m) which agrees with modern estimates. Owen incorporated much of Mantell's detailed work into his own report without nearly as

much creditation as there should have been, and so Mantell was gradually edged out of the story.

The discovery of a new *Iguanodon* fossil, preserving that part of the spine adjoining the pelvis, showed Owen that the backbones were fused in a similar fashion to those of *Megalosaurus*. For Owen this was further proof still that the extinct forms could be grouped together and yet set apart from other reptile groups. He added these conclusions to his report as he prepared it for publication: 'the combination of such characters... altogether peculiar among Reptiles... will, it is presumed, be deemed sufficient ground for establishing a distinct tribe or suborder of Saurian Reptiles for which I would propose the name of *Dinosauria*'.

This additional work behind closed doors allowed Owen to 'steal a march' on Mantell and Buckland. By coining this single word, which means 'terrible', 'awesome' or 'fearfully great lizard', Owen provided an icon that effectively revolutionised our view of the geological past and its life. But his master stroke in spreading the 'word' took another 10 years to achieve. His BAAS report was published in April 1842 (although some copies went out misdated as August 1841, which confused many later historians of science).

Owen soon began reaping the rewards. At the beginning of November 1842 he was offered a civil list pension of £200 a year, which helped guarantee his independence and ability to continue his researches without having to spend too much time on mundane tasks such as teaching to earn his daily bread and butter, unlike poor Mantell.

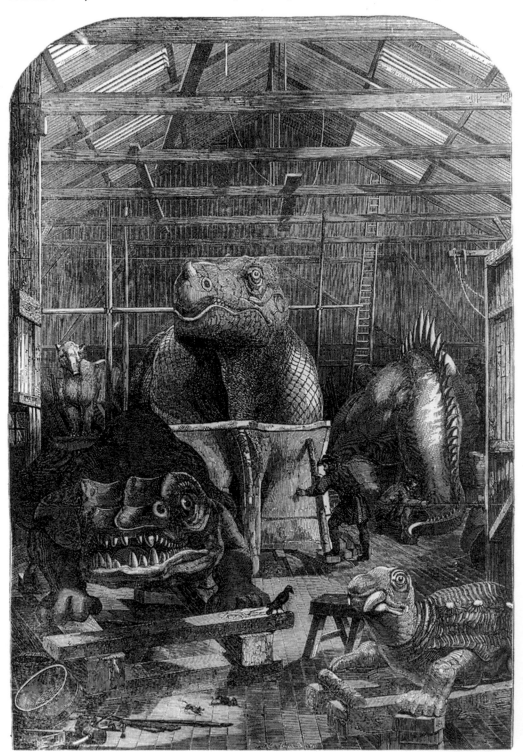

LEFT:
Waterhouse Hawkins's Crystal Palace workshop in south London and the construction of the first life-sized models of dinosaurs and other extinct vertebrates as shown in the Illustrated London News

Mantell struggled on, despite the growing deformity of his spine. With new specimens, he described new saurians (or dinosaurs as they were now called), including the first of the giant sauropods, *Cetiosaurus*. In fact Owen had named this beast because some of its bone structure looked like that of whales, so he thought that it was aquatic and not a dinosaur. Mantell managed to score over Owen by showing that the animal was in fact a dinosaur. Mantell finally got some compensatory credit for all his efforts in the form of the Royal Medal of the Royal Society in 1849.

The world's first theme park

Within a decade of inventing the dinosaurs Owen made what must be one of the biggest coups in terms of scientific publicity in the whole of the 19th century. He redefined the concept and appearance of his invention and transformed Mantell's 'lowly, creeping', serpent-like creature into something much more ponderous and imperious as befitted the new Victorian era. *Iguanodon* was remodelled as a curious chimaera with a stance rather like a mammalian rhinoceros, legs brought close in to the body to support the huge bulky body, with massive tail and head. It was given a typical reptilian scaly skin and a rather baleful stare, curiously like Queen Victoria in her old age. Owen calculated that his *Iguanodon* might be as much as six times the size of an elephant but that was before 'dinoflation' set in.

It was the relocation of Thomas Paxton's world-famous Crystal Palace from the 1851 Great Exhibition site in Kensington to Sydenham in south London that gave Owen his opportunity. With his royal connections and the ear of Prince Albert, Owen grasped his chance to put his concept of the dinosaur into practice by recreating them as life-size models. The whole scheme was very ambitious, with a 'greenfield' site landscaped with real rock strata, a lake with fossil crocodiles, and an island on which the dinosaurs were to be 'safely' marooned and surrounded by appropriate vegetation. Apart from *Iguanodon* there were two other dinosaurs – *Hyleosaurus* and *Megalosaurus* – and even more ancient amphibian labyrinthodont and younger Tertiary and Quaternary mammals, altogether representing a broad sweep of ancient life. But the ancient menagerie was never completed; there was a planned life-size restoration of an American mastodon, but funds were cut off by the Crystal Palace company.

The models were created by the artist Benjamin Waterhouse Hawkins (1810–89), under Owen's supervision, and the construction process was closely trailed and illustrated by the popular journals of the day. On New Year's Day 1853 a celebratory seven-course dinner for the great and the good of the day was held within the cast of the *Iguanodon*, surrounded by a panoply of heroes' names: Buckland, Cuvier, Owen and Mantell. The

RIGHT:
Waterhouse Hawkins's ambitious plan for his life-size models and their setting at the Crystal Palace which was partly fulfilled and is still there today

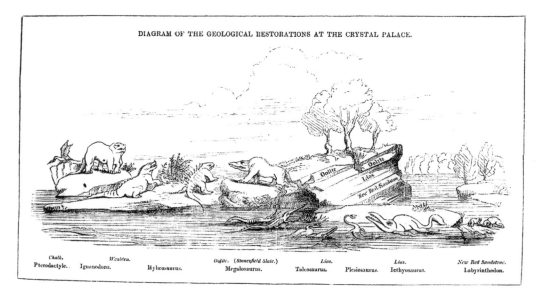

DIAGRAM OF THE GEOLOGICAL RESTORATIONS AT THE CRYSTAL PALACE.

Chalk.	Wealden.		Oolite. (Stonesfield Slate.)	Lias.	Lias.	New Red Sandstone.
Pterodactyle.	Iguanodons.	Hyleosaurus.	Megalosaurus.	Teleosaurus.	Plesiosaurus.	Iethyosaurus.	Labyrinthodon.

idea may have come from another earlier famous fossil dinner in 1801, held in his Philadelphia museum by American artist and museum owner Charles Willson Peale. Dinner for 12 was held inside the partly reconstructed skeleton of a mastodon, which Peale had excavated. Patriotic toasts were made, with rousing choruses of *Yankee Doodle*.

The Crystal Palace invitation card, drawn by Hawkins, had its text written on the outstretched wing of a flying reptile. Again the occasion was pictured in the *London Illustrated News*, giving further publicity to the project. Attended by the likes of Charles Lyell, there was an elaborately amusing 'fossiliferous' menu and a special song composed for the occasion.

> *A thousand ages underground,*
> *His skeleton had lain,*
> *But now his body's big and round*
> *And there's life in him again!*
>
> *His bones like Adam's wrapped in clay*
> *his ribs of iron stout,*
> *where is the brute alive today*
> *That dares turn him out.*
>
> *Beneath his hide he's got inside*
> *The souls of living men,*
> *Who dares our Saurian now deride*
> *With life in him again?*

Chorus:
The jolly old beast
Is not deceased
There's life in him again!

The chorus presumably referred to the dinosaur, but it may also have been a dig at Owen. He managed to sound the only sour note of the evening by publicly attacking Hawkins for 'getting the *Iguanodon* wrong', which was a bit rich considering he was supposed to have been supervising the construction. Owen was probably covering his own back, as recently fossil footprints had been found which suggested that *Iguanodon* walked upright on its two hind legs. Owen seems to have been a thoroughly unpleasant man, generally disliked by his contemporaries; nevertheless his anatomical talent does have to be acknowledged.

The grand reopening of the Crystal Palace at Sydenham on 10 June 1854 by Queen Victoria drew a crowd of 40,000. The first theme park in the world was open to an incredulous public, and it went on to draw an average 2 million visitors a year until the end of the century. More engraved illustrations were reproduced in the popular press, including *Punch*, the famous satirical magazine of the day. Here, a Victorian top-hatted father is portrayed, intent on improving his young son's mind by visiting the antediluvian reptiles. The child is screaming with horror; unperturbed, the father walks on and the punch line reads, 'Master Tom strongly objects to having his mind improved'. The giant models have recently been renovated and are still to be seen at Sydenham, although Paxton's wonderful Crystal Palace was unfortunately burned down in 1936.

News of the huge success of the venture soon spread and Hawkins was invited to New York for a repeat performance in Central Park. He set up his studio and began producing an even more ambitious scheme with many more fossil reconstructions. Unfortunately, it fell foul of local politics and came to nothing, although some of the completed models are reputed to have been broken up and buried in the park. Despite some modern searches nothing has been turned up.

However, the impetus for dinosaur research had taken off in America in a big way, and with this the whole concept of the dinosaur was to change radically. As we have seen, the new American image that was to emerge for the dinosaurs began back at the beginning of the century when Pliny Moody uncovered fossil footprints on the family farm in Massachusetts. A local naturalist, Edward Hitchcock, eventually described them in 1836 and concluded that they had been made by some large, three-toed animals. At the time the only known animals to produce such tracks were birds, and Hitchcock concluded that giant birds made the tracks. What he had found was actually the first evidence that some dinosaurs were not four-legged, as Owen and everyone else had at first assumed. As

we now know, Hitchcock was partly right; some dinosaurs were indeed built like giant two-legged birds. *Iguanodon* was one of these three-toed bipedal monsters, but the connection was not made until 1878, when Belgian miners came across the skeletons of some 40 *Iguanodon*. Sadly, Mantell did not live to see how his dinosaur really looked. He had died 26 years earlier, in 1852.

Whilst Hitchcock's 'big birds' turned out to be dinosaurs, by the early 1860s real fossil birds were making a big impact on understanding of past life and producing vital supporting evidence for the Darwin/Wallace theory of evolution.

RIGHT:
Owen's illustration of Archaeopteryx *anatomy provided the first good example of a fossil 'link' between two classes of animals, the reptiles and the birds*

BELOW:
August Goldfuss's 1831 illustration of an extinct flying reptile recovered from the Solnhofen lithographic limestones of Bavaria

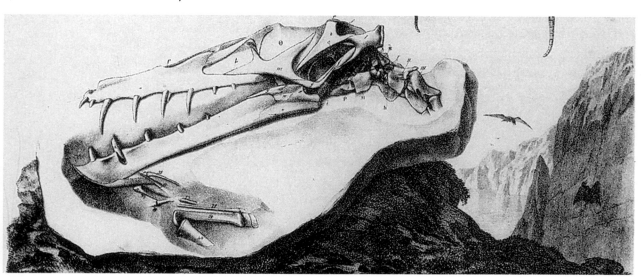

Where there's a feather there's a bird nearby

The discovery in 1860 of a small fossil feather in the Jurassic age Solnhofen limestones of Bavaria, southern Germany, was the precursor to one of the most important finds ever made in palaeontology. Feathers were regarded as unique features of birds (until very recently) and so where there was a feather there was a good chance that its bird owner would not be too far away. Six months later, in 1861, that 'owner' was found, a magpie-sized skeleton flattened in the rock. Attached to the splayed-out arms were clear impressions of asymmetric flight feathers forming remarkably modern-looking wings.

Unusually for a bird, the beak was full of teeth and there was a long, bony, feathered tail. Apart from the feathers, the only other characteristic bird feature was a bird-like boomerang-shaped wishbone. This curious chimaera or hybrid with its strange mixture of bird and reptile characteristics provided the first convincing support for the Darwin–Wallace theory of evolution from the fossil record. Called *Archaeopteryx*, meaning 'ancient wing', the fossil provided the first missing ancestral link between two major groups of animals: the reptiles and birds.

For centuries Bavaria's late Jurassic age limestones had been quarried for high-quality lithographic printing stone. Splitting the limestone into slabs often revealed exquisitely preserved fossil remains of a great variety of organisms that the quarrymen put aside to be sold to collectors. The first single feather was just 5cm (2in) long and brownish-black in colour (due to its keratin protein being carbonised during fossilisation) and preserved in remarkable detail. It is an asymmetric flight feather and even retains some downy elements near the base of the shaft, just like the advanced feathers of a modern bird.

In 1862 the complete skeleton was bought by Richard Owen of the British Museum in London. Thanks to Owen's swift action, the specimen is still amongst the most valuable fossils in the world and the Natural History Museum's most treasured possession, despite the fact that some six other *Archaeopteryx* specimens have since been found. Owen, one of the great anatomists of the day, was also a severe critic of Darwin's evolutionary ideas. Nevertheless his masterly description of the 170-million-year-old fossil showed that, whilst 'unequivocally a bird', it also had characters only found in the embryos of living birds.

However, it was the English biologist and evolutionist, Thomas Henry Huxley, who first realised that *Archaeopteryx* shows a mixture of reptilian and bird characteristics. The fossil provided something that Darwin thought the fossil record would never be able to do: it represented an ancestral link between two major groups of backboned animals. As such, it was an excellent example of Darwinian evolution and Huxley made the most of it in his proselytisation for the Darwin–Wallace theory of evolution.

Huxley knew that in the late 1850s the skeleton of a small bipedal dinosaur, *Compsognathus*, had been found at Solnhofen and that it closely resembled *Archaeopteryx*. For Huxley there was no inherent problem; even in linking separate classes of animals despite their seemingly different anatomy and physiology, it reinforced his view, as did Owen's embryological evidence. Huxley was a particularly persuasive speaker in a way that the shy and private Darwin was not. There is little doubt that a great deal of the growing acceptance of Darwin's revolutionary ideas was due to Huxley's powerful advocacy through his public lectures and published essays.

Archaeopteryx was a medium sized bird (like a magpie), about 300–500mm (11½–19½in) long from the tip of its snout to the end of its long tail, and stood some 250mm (9¾in) high. The skull is lightly constructed with large eyes and optic lobes in the brain, showing that it depended on sight as a key sense for survival. The narrow, pointed, beak-like jaws were armed with widely spaced sharp teeth. The neck is curved and leads into a short back and long, straight tail with 22 vertebrae. The forelimbs have three greatly elongate fingers, each ending in a long curved claw. The pelvis is similar to that of a small theropod reptile, but there has been some controversy over the exact form of its construction.

The question is whether the pubis was aligned vertically as in some dinosaurs, or backwards, as in living birds. Compression of specimens during fossilisation often creates such problems. The hind limbs were particularly reptile-like, with the inner toe being very short and lying at the rear of the foot. However, this condition is also typical of many living birds; as Huxley pointed out, the foot of a chicken embryo is hard to differentiate from that of a reptile.

The living habits of *Archaeopteryx* and its flying ability have also been a matter of considerable argument. It has often been portrayed as a forest inhabitant, capable of climbing trees using the hooked claws on its wing fingers and feet. Its feathers were ideal wing material, since they are light, waterproof and do not tear easily. This combination provides quite an attractive model for a prototype bird, with the animal taking to the trees to escape predators and to find food. Being able to glide from one tree canopy to another would have several advantages; it saves energy and the risks of returning to the ground all the time. Gliding could then have evolved more easily into powered flapping flight, so extending the animal's range.

One snag with this model for *Archaeopteryx* is that the environment in which the bird lived does not include any substantial trees. The only available land seems to have been some low-lying islands within the lagoon where the Solnhofen lime-rich muds accumulated. With the prevailing hot and fairly arid climate, these islands would not have been able to support tree-sized vegetation but rather a sparse low scrub of bushes separated by open ground. The plant fossils from the same deposit support this reconstruction, since they lack any wood and only preserve the remains of some small shrubby conifers *Brachyphyllum* and *Palaeocyparis* and bennettitalean plants, which only grew to about 3m (10ft) high.

Nevertheless, there is no doubt that *Archaeopteryx* was capable of climbing and flying. The primary wing feathers are asymmetric and that means one thing only – flight, even if it was fairly clumsy and inefficient. Modern flightless birds do not have asymmetric feathers.

Archaeopteryx relationships

It was one thing to recognise the reptile relationships of *Archaeopteryx* but quite another to determine which reptilian group it is closest to. In recent years the possibilities have ranged from links with crocodiles, thecodont reptiles, mammals or dinosaurs. The crocodile link was based on certain similarities in skull structure but these are common to other archosaur reptiles and difficult to match exactly. The link with the thecodont reptiles of Triassic times was based on general similarities and the bird-like proportions of some of these early reptiles, but again close ties have not been convincingly established. The mammal link was interesting and based on both groups being warm-blooded, with four chambered hearts, advanced brains and insulation made from the protein keratin (bird feathers and mammalian hair). There are a number of other similarities but no supporting fossil evidence, and many of the seemingly shared characters are hard to defend in detail.

The strongest link is with the dinosaurs. Another specimen of *Archaeopteryx* was found by American palaeontologist John Ostrom in the Tyler Museum in Haarlem, Holland, catalogued as the small dinosaur *Compsognathus* because the faint impressions of feathers were not spotted when the specimen was first acquired.

Ostrom has listed dozens of similarities between the skeletons of *Archaeopteryx* and those of advanced theropod dinosaurs such as the two-legged *Deinonychus*. He concluded that birds are specialised coelurosaurs. In retrospect it is not surprising that specimens of *Archaeopteryx* could be mistaken for dinosaurs since, apart from their feathers, they virtually *are* dinosaurs.

Fluffy dinosaurs?

This association between birds and dinosaurs has been spectacularly confirmed in recent years. In one way you could argue the dinosaurs have not become extinct but are very much still with us; they are now covered in feathers and we call them birds. Over the last decade the picture of dinosaur–bird relationships has become even more intriguing. Feathers have always been considered to be a unique characteristic of the birds, but a series of astonishing fossil discoveries in early Cretaceous strata of China has shown

RIGHT:
Louis Figuier's 1865 reconstruction of life in late Jurassic times with accurately depicted land plants and the earliest reconstruction of the long-tailed Archaeopteryx *bird in flight*

otherwise. Firstly, two small bipedal theropod dinosaurs (*Protarchaeopteryx* and *Caudipteryx*) have been found with traces of feathers attached to their bodies. These animals could not fly and were not birds, but they were still dinosaurs.

In 1996 another Chinese specimen of similar age, *Sinosauropteryx* (very similar to the small theropod dinosaur *Compsognathus* and to the bird *Archaeopteryx*) was found, with a crest of small feather-like structures running down its neck, backbone and flanks. So unusual did the structures seem that many experts dismissed them as peculiar preservational features. However, it is now clear that this animal has to be included in the 'fold' of feathered dinosaurs.

At the end of 2000 yet another Chinese find, *Microraptor*, hit the news. This is the smallest adult dinosaur yet discovered, being no more than the size of a crow. The specimen had a curiously troubled history as it started life as a fake, smuggled out of China and sold in America on the commercial market. The quality of the forgery was good enough to fool a number of experts and end up on the pages of the *National Geographic* magazine in 1999, portrayed as *Archaeoraptor*; yet another 'missing link', this time between dinosaurs and birds.

As the name suggests, with its more bird-like body and dinosaur tail plus feathers, it was thought to be even closer than *Archaeopteryx* to the gap between the two groups. Inevitably there was serious money behind the 'scam'; unique fossils can command 'big bucks' these days. Someone knew exactly what they were doing and what would really tempt the experts to suspend their full critical faculties and part with a lot of money. Fortunately there were enough experts who were suspicious and the forgery was soon revealed, but not before the prestigious *National Geographic* had tarnished its reputation. X-ray computed tomography (CT) showed that the slab had been cobbled together from numerous broken pieces and mounted on a single slab.

The good news was that the forgery was made up of parts of genuine specimens, maybe as many as five, some of which were very interesting in their own right. One turned out to be a primitive bird skeleton

and the other a new dinosaur that has now been reassembled as it should be and re-emerged into the scientific limelight with its new name, *Microraptor*. This tiny dinosaur was also feathered, with contour feathers covering the body. More important is the additional evidence that it may also have had true shafted feathers like modern birds. Like *Archaeopteryx*, its feet had curved claws that may well have been used for perching in trees; and being so light (the body is only 47mm/under 2in long) it could well have been an adept climber. Such a reduction in size would also have been a prerequisite for the evolution of flight and supports the idea that flight was initially promoted by 'tree down' gliding rather than 'ground up' flapping. Other bird-like dinosaurs such as the 2m (6½ ft) long *Velociraptor* would have been far too big and heavy to represent the intermediate 'hop, step and jump' towards flight. Expert opinion is divided on the issue as to whether the *Microraptor* skeleton is a dromaeosaur or a troodontid.

It is becoming increasingly clear that there was evolution of carnivorous dinosaurs through the coelurosaur dinosaurs (including forms with downy feathers), maniraptoran dinosaurs (with a sideways flexing wrist, longer arms and hands, and feathers with shaft, vanes and barbs) into true birds (with arms at least as long as legs, and long flight feathers). Some experts now place the advanced maniraptoran (dromaeosurid and troodontid) dinosaurs in a group called the Paraves, but the classification is still very contentious.

Questions remain about the adaptational function of these early feathers if they were not for flight. Their sparse distribution in *Sinosauropteryx* seems to rule out insulation but camouflage, display and/or species recognition are possibilities. The feathers of *Protarchaeopteryx* and *Caudipteryx* are even more puzzling as they have some characteristics of flight feathers but could not have been used for that purpose. *Protarchaeopteryx* preserves indications of a body and tail covering of downy feathers with vaned and barbed symmetrical feathers forming a fan at the end of the tail. By comparison *Caudipteryx* has shorter arms with primary feathers

attached to the second, longest finger of the hand. These feathers are also vaned and barbed, and seem to have smaller down feathers associated with them. However, the feathers of *Archaeopteryx* are now less problematic, since they no longer appear out of the blue as fully formed flight feathers without antecedents. Although the Chinese feathered dinosaurs are stratigraphically younger in age than *Archaeopteryx*, from the evolutionary point of view they can be seen as precursors.

Within 10 million years of the appearance of *Archaeopteryx*, bird body size shrank to that of a sparrow, well below that of the smallest non-avian coelurosaurs with modifications imposed by the flying habit such as a fully opposable hallux (thumb) on the pes (foot) that allowed perching. Again, early Cretaceous deposits of China have 'come up trumps' with literally thousands of specimens of the crow-sized *Confuciusornis*, the earliest beaked (ornithurine) bird. The form of the horny beak with its slight upturn at the tip suggests that it was a plant eater. Although it has a curious mosaic of primitive *Archaeopteryx*-like features, these are outnumbered by much more modern ones such as the loss of teeth with the evolution of a horny beak and fusion of the posterior vertebrae to form a pygostyle to which long tail feathers were attached.

It is thought that *Confuciusornis* lived in large flocks alongside a freshwater lake, surrounded by lush forest. The long tail feathers of the males and the structure of the foot suggest that it did not spend much time on the ground but was a perching bird. Analysis also indicates that there were at least two species of the genus; the same is probably true for *Archaeopteryx*. Furthermore, other new finds mean that diversification amongst these early birds could have happened much earlier than previously thought. There were probably many other birds around in early Cretaceous times for which we have no fossils – yet.

Forming feathers

The origin of feathers has long been a topic of debate, but the discoveries of Chinese feathered dinosaurs has reinvigorated the whole business. Birds use feathers not just for flying but also essentially for insulation; being warm-blooded creatures they need to conserve energy as much as possible. Feathers are also remarkably tough, physically and chemically, whilst still being light and replaceable. They help protect the body and waterproof it, and have a very important function for sexual display and camouflage. So, which of these functions came first?

Modern feathers are remarkably sophisticated structures and come in three main forms: small fluffy down feathers for insulation; small hair-like filoplumes; and bigger contour feathers that cover the body and wings. Basically, feathers consist of a basal hollow quill from which the feather or vane develops as an elongate central solid shaft with numerous barbs branching out on either side. In turn, the barbs branch into numerous overlapping and interlocking barbules with hooks and notches that help hold the feather together. When birds preen they are checking this complex arrangement and realigning any displacement or damage to the various elements.

Clearly such sophisticated structures cannot have arisen fully formed. They are thought to have evolved from reptilian body scales in stages. Firstly there was scale elongation, perhaps as seen in a Triassic gliding reptile, *Longisquama*; then evolution of the central shaft, presumably as a strengthening adaptation; then differentiation of the barbs and barbules. *Archaeopteryx*'s feathers were already at the most advanced stage of evolution. By comparison *Protopteryx*, another of the recent Chinese finds, retains a feather type without barbs at the proximal end that has not been described before.

Since 1995 understanding of the early bird evolution and their relationship with the dinosaurs has been revolutionised by spectacular new fossil finds in early Cretaceous strata of China's Liaoning province. The diversity of several dozen new birds reinforces the view that early bird evolution must predate *Archaeopteryx* by some time. The 1999 discovery of feathered dromaeosaur dinosaurs such as *Sinornithosaurus* and *Microraptor* supports the idea that birds are indeed 'just' a group of feathered dinosaurs.

Chapter 6

Rock of ages – dating rocks and fossils

Radiometric dating

One of the major problems that the investigation of the geological past faced was that of chronological dating of strata and the fossils contained within them. The mapping, sequencing and correlation of strata allowed for no more than a relative dating. By Darwin's day there was also a general sense that the history of the Earth had to extend back over many hundreds of millions of years but there was no hard evidence, and influential physicists such as William Thomson, Lord Kelvin (1824–1907), doubted such long timescales. A reliable method for dating rocks did not emerge until the beginning of the 20th century.

In 1907 an American radiochemist, Bertram Boltwood (1870–1927), made a systematic analysis of radioactive uranium-bearing rocks, from which he noticed that generally both helium and lead were present, with the lead being the stable end product of the decay chain from uranium. He went on to develop a technique that allowed him to measure the ratio of radioactive isotopes of uranium and lead in a mineral from Glastonbury, Connecticut. Boltwood calculated that the rock was some 410 million years old (Ma). Although this was later redated to 265 Ma, Boltwood's technical developments, building on Ernest Rutherford's (1871–1937) pioneering work, provided the first reasonably accurate means of dating

the formation of certain minerals within the Earth.

Boltwood had studied at Yale and then in Germany. On returning to America he worked to improve the analytical techniques of radiochemistry, pioneered by his friend Rutherford. The latter had experimented on a piece of uranium ore and, in 1902, calculated that the ore had been formed 700 million years ago. If correct, this measure seemed to increase the age of the Earth hugely. But over the next few years it was realised that Rutherford's method was flawed because it relied on measuring the gas helium, which can easily escape from the rock.

By 1910 a British geologist, Arthur Holmes (1890–1965), was pursuing a similar approach and calculated the age of a Norwegian rock, containing several radioactive minerals, as 370 Ma. As the rock was known to have originated within the Devonian geological system, he thus provided the first date for that system and period of time. In retrospect this was the most accurate of the early radiometric dates and, if Holmes had had the resources to continue his work, radiometric dating would have progressed much faster than it did. Holmes also recalculated some of Boltwood's published data and arranged them to produce the first geological timescale. He was to improve on this scale continuously for the rest of his professional life.

By 1946 Holmes had made isotope measurements on some ancient lead-ore-bearing rocks from Invigtut in Greenland. These gave an age of 3,015 Ma, the first really reliable estimate of a minimum age for the Earth. Holmes went on to estimate that the origin of the uranium, from which the lead was derived, must be around 4,460 million years ago; but he thought that that origin was within the gas cloud from which the Earth was formed, rather than being the date of the Earth's origin.

By the 1950s American scientists Harrison Brown and Claire Patterson, who had worked on the Manhattan Project and the development of the atomic bomb,

became interested in using meteorites to calculate the age of the solar system. In 1953 Patterson (1922–95) managed to determine the lead isotope content of the Canyon Diablo meteorite, which blasted Meteor Crater in Arizona around 50,000 years ago. From this he calculated an age of 4,510 Ma and compared it with an age of 4,560 Ma calculated for lead values from earthbound granite and basalt rocks. He concluded that the similarity between the dates indicated that this was also the date at which the Earth first formed.

By 1956 Patterson had made further measures from different meteorites and deep-sea sediments that represented a generalised sample of Earth rocks. Again, the average worked out at 4.55 billion (= thousand million = Ba) years ago, very close to Holmes's figure.

By 1947 Holmes's development of the geological time chart allowed him to publish a graph based on the calculated radiometric ages of a number of rocks that could each be fairly accurately tied into the known succession of strata within certain geological periods. Even so there were only five reliably dated points between the Cambrian and present, ranging back as far as 450 million years to a point in mid Cambrian times. However, a curve drawn between the points allowed the first rough estimates of the duration of each geological period to be made.

A major difficulty is that most minerals

ABOVE:
Arthur Holmes, British pioneer of radioactive dating, who helped establish the first radiometric timescale for Earth history

RIGHT:
Claire Patterson, the American scientist who, in 1953, first accurately calculated the age of the Earth at around 4.5 billion years, using radioactive isotopes from rocks

that can be dated by radiometric dating are formed from an initially molten state within igneous rocks. Consequently igneous rocks are the only ones that can be reliably dated, and even then there are error bars attached to all these dates. The problem for stratigraphers (who study the history of deposition of the sedimentary strata of the Earth) and palaeontologists (who study the fossils such rocks contain) is how to relate the formation of igneous rocks to the deposition of sediments.

Stratigraphically the most useful igneous rocks are volcanic – lavas and ash deposits – that can be found interbedded with fossiliferous sediments. The problem is that the most common isotopes found within volcanic rocks are those of potassium (K) and argon (Ar), which have shorter half-lives than uranium (U) and lead (Pb). Nevertheless, K–Ar and U–Pb dating of volcanic rocks has proved immensely useful in dating Tertiary age strata, especially those associated with the Great East African Rift Valley and their human-related fossils. Whenever you see a date in years attached to some human-related fossil species, the chances are that it has been derived from some volcanic rock layer near where the fossil was found.

Without radiometric dates we would not be able to say anything about rates of geological or biological processes in the past. Prior to the late 1940s most dating of rocks and geological time was little more than informed guesswork. A sense of age for rocks and fossils was a major problem ever since the 17th century when a number of spuriously accurate estimates were made for the age of the Earth. In Europe these calculations were inevitably based on the assumption that the Old Testament was a reliable historical document. The most famous scholarly attempt to work out the date of Creation was made by James Ussher (1581–1656), Protestant Archbishop of Armagh, Ireland.

4004BC *and all that*

Ussher's was just one of many such calculations. He had the prestige of being a renowned scholar, professor of Divinity and vice-chancellor of Trinity College, Dublin. He used not only Old Testament sources but also contemporary knowledge of the Julian calendar, devised by the Renaissance scholar Joseph Justus Scaliger, astronomical calculation and extra-biblical sources. Scaliger's Julian period was taken to have started on a hypothetical day, 1 January 4713BC, which he thought predated all known historical events. According to Ussher's 1650 *Annals of the old covenant from the first origin of the world*, the world began the night before Sunday 23 October in year 710 of the Julian calendar – 4,004 years before the birth of Christ.

However, as long ago as the 5th century biblical scholars had noticed that there were problems with the Old Testament account, such as the creation of light before the creation of the Sun (Genesis 1:3, 16) and the fact that the moon is not light emitting but light reflecting. It was also long recognised that there are different components to the Genesis account. In addition, growing scholarly interest in the Classical world and the Middle East during the 18th century led to a reassessment of prehistory and a questioning of the Old Testament chronology. Nevertheless, for the majority of believers the idea that the Creation took just six days also became firmly entrenched in Western culture. By the end of the 18th century, however, there were a number of more scientific attempts to calculate the Earth's age.

The French natural philosopher and experimenter, Comte de Buffon (1707–88), mustered a number of lines of evidence to support his ideas about the cooling of the Earth and the time it had taken to do so: in other words, the age of the Earth. The existence of the bones and tusks of elephants in far northern latitudes such as Siberia indicated to de Buffon that in earlier times the Earth must have been as hot as Africa. By 1778 de Buffon divided earth history into seven epochs, echoing the days of Creation in the Genesis narrative, with man only appearing in the last epoch, suggesting to Buffon that there was a substantially long period of prehistory or prehuman time.

De Buffon also tried an experimental approach, building on ideas developed by Isaac Newton. Heating a number of iron balls of different sizes to white heat, de Buffon timed how long they took to cool.

Georges-Louis Leclerc, Comte de Buffon, the 18th-century French aristocrat and experimenter who tried to estimate the age of the Earth by calculating the time it would have taken to cool from being red-hot to its surface being habitable – some 60,000 years

He found that Newton's conjecture that the cooling time was proportional to the diameter of the sphere was correct. However, de Buffon disagreed with Newton over the cooling time of an iron ball the size of the Earth and reckoned that it would have taken 96,670 years and 132 days, almost twice as long as Newton's calculation.

De Buffon was not entirely satisfied with the result. He was aware that the Earth was made of other materials with different cooling rates and that the Sun contributed heat to the Earth, which would have prolonged its cooling time. By 1779 he arrived at his final calculation of 74,832 years for the age of the Earth. De Buffon reckoned that some 60,000 years had passed before the Earth was cool enough to be inhabited and then steamy jungles had stretched as far north as Siberia; it was not fit for humans for another 10,000 years. According to de Buffon 'thus we are persuaded, independently of the authority of the sacred books, that man has been created last, and that he arrived to take the sceptre of the earth only when it was found worthy of his empire'.

Despite Newton and de Buffon's work, Ussher's 4004BC date was still widely accepted and even printed in bibles as an historic truth. Not surprisingly, the notion of a 6,000-year-old Earth persisted into the 19th century and beyond as an established 'fact' for some fundamentalist Christians. It was still being quoted in the infamous 1925 Scopes trial between American creationists and evolutionists in Dayton, Ohio.

By the latter part of the 18th century, James Hutton (1726–97), the Scottish natural philosopher, showed from his study of stratification and rates of sedimentation that Ussher's 6,000 years was not nearly enough time for observed rates of geological processes. Hutton proclaimed from his examination of strata that he could see 'no vestige of a beginning, no prospect of an end'. By the latter part of the 19th century, Lyell and Darwin were using rates of erosion and deposition to estimate that the Earth was hundreds of millions of years old.

Such geological efforts were severely criticised by the physicist Lord Thomson. From known melting points for rocks, Kelvin modelled Earth evolution as a process of thermal diffusion that, according to his calculations, took some 20 million years to create a thickened crust from an initially molten state. Such was Kelvin's influence that his measures were readily accepted by most scientists apart from some geologists who still thought that they were a serious underestimate. As the role of radioactivity was not known, Kelvin's measure was indeed a serious underestimate. It is often stated that the discovery of radioactivity and its role in maintaining the internal temperature of the Earth finally broke the straitjacket of Kelvin's influence. This view fails to take into account Kelvin's dogmatism in linking the age of the Earth to that of the Sun. Ideas about solar energy and the Sun's compositional homogeneity were not overthrown by the discovery of radioactivity. The paradox was not fully resolved until the recognition of thermonuclear fusion in the 1930s.

It is now known that the early formation of the Earth, as part of the accretionary disc around the Sun, began 4.57 Ba. Earth's early growth was protracted, being dominated by planetary collisions, and it was not until around 4.51–4.45 Ba that it reached its present mass, with a metal core and primitive atmosphere. At present the Earth's oldest known rock material is a 4.4-Ba zircon crystal from Australia, dated by an Australian/American team in January 2001, using the uranium–lead (U–Pb) method. Zircon is a particularly tough and enduring mineral, resilient to change, and generally formed in continental crust rocks. The composition of the zircon suggested to the researchers that the Earth's early growth was protracted over 100 Ma and that there must have been continental crust and water on the Earth's surface by 4.3 Ba, much earlier than previously thought. However, most of the Earth's geological record extends back no more than 4 Ba, to the end of the early intense phase of meteorite bombardment, which destroyed or reworked almost all the older material.

How ancient is life?

Today, Earth's 4.6-billion-year history is divided into two major eons: the Phanerozoic (meaning 'evident life') and Precambrian or Cryptozoic (meaning 'hidden life'). During the 545 million years of Phanerozoic time, which begins with the Cambrian Period, abundant life is recorded by fossils with preservable hard parts. The 4 billion and more years of Precambrian time seemed to be devoid of any persistently convincing traces of life until 1953 when American geologist Stanley Tyler discovered 2.1-billion-year-old Precambrian microfossils in ancient Canadian rocks.

As Charles Darwin suspected a hundred years earlier, that discovery demonstrated that there was a missing Precambrian record of life. Darwin was puzzled by the way fossils representing 'several of the main divisions of the animal kingdom suddenly appear in the lowest known [Cambrian] fossiliferous rocks'. He was particularly

worried because 'if the theory [of evolution] be true, it is indisputable that before the lowest Cambrian stratum was deposited, long periods elapsed... and that during these vast periods, the world swarmed with living creatures...' He could 'give no satisfactory explanation' as to why pre-Cambrian fossils were not being found. It seemed to him that 'the case at present must remain inexplicable; and may be truly urged as a valid argument against the views here entertained [his theory of evolution]'. Today it is generally thought that life began on Earth at least 3.8 billion years ago, and perhaps as long ago as 4 billion years ago.

The question of when life on Earth began and what the earliest life forms were like has great importance for our understanding of the evolution of life, but has proved very difficult to answer. A number of problems prevent palaeontologists from providing a simple answer, but at least we are getting much closer to doing so. There is now fossil evidence for life on Earth stretching back deep into Archean (early Precambrian) times. Less than a hundred years ago the fossil evidence only extended back to the earliest Cambrian strata, which we now know to be no more than 545 million years old.

Different approaches to this particular quest have been taken over recent years. Palaeontologists now claim that, despite the problems of fossil preservation and the gappy nature of the fossil record, especially within the vast chronological stretch of the 4-billion-year-long Precambrian, it is still worth looking for fossil evidence of early life; and they claim to have found various clues in rocks that are around 3.8 billion years old.

Fossils of ancient life?

Biologists tend to dismiss the potential of the fossil record because, at best, it can only provide petrified and generally fragmented remains, for which few biological characters can be determined. They prefer to search among the most primitive life forms alive today to see if they can get some idea of what the first organisms might have been like. In recent years more and more primitive organisms, generally known as extremophiles, have been found surviving under the most rigorous conditions of heat, cold, pressure, acidity and alkalinity. These organisms, mostly microbial, have extended our understanding of the limits to life. We now know that life can tolerate environmental conditions ranging from the deepest parts of dark, cold and pressurised ocean waters to living in polar ice, hot acid geysers, alkaline lakes and the hottest deserts. These extreme conditions are thought to approach those that existed in the early stages of Earth's development. Environments for life were then very different to those that most life forms, especially the more complex ones, can tolerate today.

Likewise biochemists, from their studies of the basic biochemical prerequisites for primitive organisms, have speculated upon how such life forms might originate. They have also successfully experimented with the synthesis of the basic building blocks for life, the giant organic molecules known as amino acids.

The gradual plumbing of the geological depths of the stratigraphic rock record in the early part of the 19th century revolutionised ideas about how strata might be subdivided and how fossil remains were distributed through the rocks. Nevertheless, it is still surprising to discover that, as little as 150 years ago, scientists did not know about life's long 'fuse' prior to the Cambrian explosion. It became evident that

Transition rocks were fossiliferous and, as we have seen, by 1835 Murchison and Sedgwick had subdivided them into Silurian and Cambrian.

Ancient life moves to Ireland – Oldhamia

The discovery in 1844 of a strange trace fossil in the 4.5km (2¾-mile) thick Cambrian rock strata from Bray Head, south of Dublin, and its description by Edward Forbes (1815–54) in 1848, opened up the argument about primitive forms of life. Forbes named the small branching and radiating marks in these ancient seabed mudrocks *Oldhamia* after Thomas Oldham, professor of geology in Trinity College, Dublin, the geologist who first found them. Based on a superficial resemblance, Forbes suggested that *Oldhamia* might be the remains of a bryozoan, but no skeletal remains or other indications of affinity with such moss-animals were to be seen. Since no shelly fossils were found associated with these trace fossils at Bray, the relative position of the strata was not clear and there was no particular progression in the argument.

Oldhamia has since been found associated with known Cambrian fossils from around Boston, Massachusetts, in New York State and with the important Cambrian trilobite *Paradoxides* in the Oslo region of Norway. Other trace fossils, such as *Arenicolites* and *Skolithos*, have since been found in the Bray rocks and, along with *Oldhamia*, are all seen as the burrows and feeding traces of some small soft bodied worm-like organisms.

And then Canada – Eozoon

New ground was broken a couple of decades later in 1858, when some organic-looking remains were found in limestones exposed along the Ottawa River, west of Montreal in Canada. They were the first putative fossils to be found in these ancient Laurentian rocks (now known to be about 1.1 billion years old). The layered structures looked organic, having a cross-section showing flattened oval vesicles, some of which were interconnected with branching filamentous structures. It was

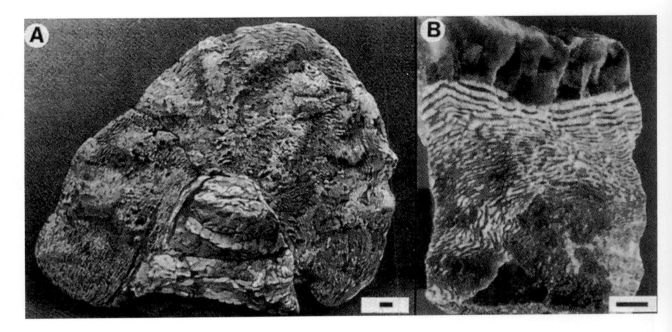

interpreted, in 1865, as a giant protozoan by John William Dawson (1820–99). A student of Charles Lyell and fellow Scot, Dawson had emigrated to Canada and became one of North America's best-known palaeontologists. He called the fossil *Eozoon canadense*, meaning 'dawn animal from Canada', and suggested that it was the oldest and most primitive organism known.

In 1870 the evolutionary biologist Thomas Henry Huxley hailed *Eozoon* as supporting evidence for his (and Darwin's) claim that there must have been a prolonged and almost unrecorded succession of primitive life forms in Precambrian rocks. Even the fossil fish from Silurian strata, the oldest fish known at the time, were already well-advanced forms, a long way 'down the road' from their evolutionary origins. Hugh Miller had made much of this fact and used it to try and counter evolutionary arguments several decades before. But Huxley was undeterred by such arguments and perceptively remarked that 'it is appalling to speculate upon the extent to which that origin must have preceded the epoch of the first recorded appearance of vertebrate life'.

Dawson was, like Miller, a strict and fairly fundamental Calvinist and against the idea of evolution. He thought quite the reverse, that *Eozoon* demonstrated that 'there is no link whatever in the geological fact to connect *Eozoon* with the Mollusks, Radiates, or crustaceans of the succeeding

ABOVE:
Eozoon canadense, the 'dawn animal of Canada', as illustrated by Dawson in 1875 and believed to be the oldest fossil (the bar is 1cm long)

LEFT:
Dawson's detailed reconstruction of Eozoon *as a Precambrian protozoan. It has since been shown to be inorganic*

[Cambrian rock strata]... these stand before us as distinct creations. [A] gap... yawns in our imperfect geological record. Of actual facts, therefore, we have none; and those evolutionists who have regarded the dawn-animal as an evidence in their favour, have been obliged to have recourse to supposition and assumption'.

Not everyone agreed with Dawson's identification; it was pointed out that his so-called 'protozoan' was far bigger than any living forms. Despite being supported by William Carpenter (1813–85), a leading protozoologist, the argument rumbled on. William King, the Irish-based palaeontologist, who first named the Neanderthals as a distinct and separate human species, constantly seems to have been on the lookout for any opportunity to make a 'splash'. In 1866 King speculatively argued that he could find no convincing organic signs in the published illustrations of *Eozoon canadense* and regarded the structure as purely mineralogical.

Dawson staunchly fought his corner over the years, but in 1894, just a few years before his death, *Eozoon*-like structures were found in limestone blocks ejected from Vesuvius. King was right; the structures were inorganic and resulted from the metamorphism of minerals making up the limestone. Meanwhile, back in North America, the search for ancient life continued in new fields. Charles Doolittle Walcott (1850–1927) was to become the most important palaeontologist in America thanks to his unusual combination of talents as a field geologist, finder and describer of important fossils and scientific administrator. He is best known in palaeontological circles for discovering and excavating the Cambrian age Burgess Shale and its fossil riches.

Walcott started off his professional life as assistant to James Hall (1811–98), the famously irascible chief geologist of New York State, who sent him out investigate some curious mound-shaped structures in Cambrian limestones near Saratoga, New York State. Hall suspected the structures were biological in origin. This introduction was to prove useful to Walcott when, as a member of the USGS, he was sent out to search for evidence of early life in Precambrian strata exposed in the bottom of the Grand Canyon. In 1883, the year in which Hall named the Saratoga fossil mounds *Cryptozoon* (meaning 'hidden life'), Walcott reported that he had found similar looking structures in the Grand Canyon. He became convinced, as he wrote in 1891, that 'the life in the [Precambrian] seas was large and varied there can be little, if any doubt' and that 'it is only a question of search and favorable conditions to discover it'.

Surprisingly it took more than 50 years before fossil evidence for Precambrian life was generally accepted, even though great thicknesses of Precambrian seabed sediments were discovered, some of which had not been metamorphosed or greatly deformed by earth movements. It was the discovery of beautifully preserved microfossils in the Gunflint Chert of Ontario, Canada, in the 1950s that led to a renaissance in the palaeontological investigation of Precambrian strata.

Biologists look for primitive life in some warm pond

Whilst geologists were discovering well-preserved Precambrian strata but still no really good fossils in the latter part of the 19th century, biologists were uncovering an astonishing diversity of life on Earth, especially amongst water-living primitive micro-organisms. They soon realised that there must have been a number of evolutionary stages as life became more complex in its organisation. Could any such stages be preserved as fossils?

In 1871 Darwin wrote to his friend and mentor, the botanist Joseph Hooker, that, 'It is often said that all of the conditions for the first production of a living organism are now present, which could ever have been present. But if (and oh! what a big if!) we could conceive in some warm pond, with all sorts of ammonia and phosphoric salts, lights, heat, electricity etc present, that a protein compound was chemically formed ready to undergo still more complex changes, at the present day such matter would be instantly devoured or absorbed, which would not have been the case before living creatures were formed'.

Alexander Ivanovich Oparin (1894–1980) was a brilliant young Russian biochemist who, in the 1920s, noticed that oils can be dispersed in water as tiny spherical droplets that, superficially at least, are like simple living cells. Oparin proposed that life was first built up of increasingly complex molecules, made from the four basic and very abundant elements – carbon, hydrogen, oxygen and nitrogen – that readily combine together. He thought that small robust molecules, such as methane (CH_4), carbon dioxide (CO_2) and ammonia (NH_3), might have combined together in water, lacking free oxygen, to form bigger and more complex molecules in a primordial soup. Over time some of these organic ingredients combined together to form enzymes and finally genes. But Oparin had little or no idea what genes really are, nor did he know what might have stimulated such an increase in complexity. It was not until 1938, when his first major book on his ideas was translated into English, that the scientific world outside Russia was alerted to Oparin's ideas.

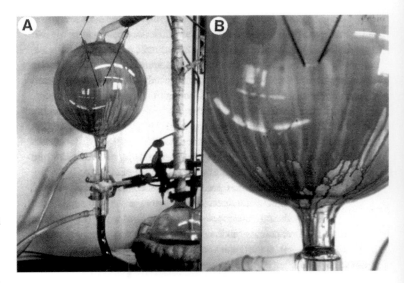

By the 1950s biochemists had a much better understanding of what the prerequisites for life might have been. Those basic elements of organic molecules – carbon, hydrogen, oxygen and nitrogen – had to be present in water at an appropriate temperature above freezing and below boiling. Most importantly there had to be energy, perhaps supplied by lightning. Stanley Miller (1930–), an American chemist, put all these 'ingredients' together in a series of lab experiments.

The result was an impressive array of organic molecules, including 25 amino acids, which are the basic building blocks of proteins. Thus the idea that life perhaps began as a 'primordial soup' of amino acids was given a considerable boost. Somehow or other this process of synthesis led on to proteins and simple living cells. But there was an essential missing ingredient. There was no obvious mechanism for the 'ratcheting' process that could have achieved this progression. Nevertheless, the experimental approach helped underpin the consensus view that a prerequisite to the early evolution of life on Earth was the synthesis of complex organic molecules.

Real Precambrian life

In March 1946 a new window into the strange world of early life was opened up. An Australian geologist, Reginald Sprigg, found some curious saucer-sized, jellyfish-like markings in what, he thought, were earliest Cambrian sandstones near an abandoned lead-zinc mine in the Ediacara

ABOVE:
Experimental equipment of the kind used by Stanley Miller in his ground-breaking trials which showed that complex organic compounds could be synthesised in the laboratory from naturally occurring gases such as methane, carbon dioxide and ammonia

Hills of the Flinders Ranges, north of Adelaide, South Australia. In his published reports, Sprigg called them *Ediacara flindersi*, noticed that they lacked hard parts and suggested that they represented some of the oldest evidence for animal life. Their importance was not to be fully appreciated for another decade or more. The Ediacaran sandstones are now known to be late Precambrian in age.

Meanwhile, in the mid 1950s an English schoolboy, Roger Mason, found some equally strange-looking, fern-like impressions on sandstone bedding planes in Charnwood Forest, Leicestershire. By contrast with the Ediacaran strata, these deposits were known to be late Precambrian in age, but their fossils were preserved in the same unusual way as the Ediacaran 'jellyfish' as a kind of trace fossil with raised surface impressions of the shape of the organism. But as there is no evident skeletal material, it was assumed that they must be soft-bodied creatures, like jellyfish and other scyphozoans.

Details of the Charnwood fossils were published in 1958 by Trevor Ford, a palaeontologist at Leicester University. The study of the Ediacaran fossils, which were more numerous and better preserved, was not fully promoted at the international level until the 1960s when they were described in the *Scientific American* by a Czech emigré to Australia, Martin Glaessner (1906–89).

Making an important discovery is not enough to guarantee its appreciation, unless it is made by someone who is already famous and has publishing access to the most important scientific journals. Publication does not necessarily help if it is in an obscure journal and the scientist is not part of an appreciative network of scientists who will promote the find.

Canada triumphs again

It was the advent of the transmission electron microscope that first revealed the remarkable preservation of really old, Precambrian, microfossils in the silica-rich chert deposits of the Gunflint Ironstone in Ontario. Stanley A. Tyler (1906–63), a prominent American economic geologist at the University of Wisconsin, set out to investigate the iron-rich Gunflint Formation strata in 1953. His task was to map out the strata and work out how they were formed.

The story goes that one Sunday in late August he went fishing near Flint Island in Lake Superior. Spotting a strange-looking outcrop of rock strata along the shore, his geological curiosity got the better of him. On landing, he saw a bedding plane exposure of recognisable Gunflint strata, stripped bare of soil and vegetation by glaciation. But here the chert, instead of being red and iron-rich, was jet-black and accompanied by large *Cryptozoon*-like mounds. He collected a number of specimens and went back to his fishing.

BELOW:
Late Precambrian fossils (Tribrachidium, Dickinsonia, Spriggina), members of the 560-million-year-old Ediacaran soft-bodied fauna from South Australia

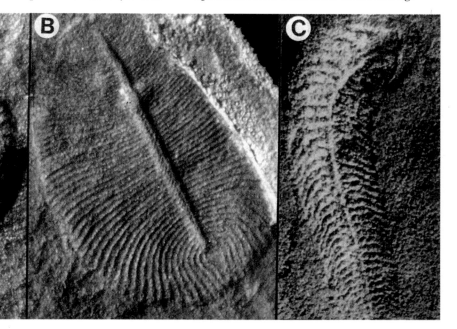

Little did he realise just what he had in his rock specimens; not until he got back to his lab was he to find out.

To investigate the structure of such finely grained crypto-crystalline cherts, Tyler had to slice the rock into sections thin enough to examine with a high-power microscope. To his amazement, the black colour of the chert was clearly caused by wispy layers of microscopic particles, myriads of micron-sized filaments and hollow spheres. Tyler knew that as the Gunflint rocks were mid-Precambrian in age they were 'seriously' old. No radiometric dates were then available for the rocks and they have subsequently been dated at 2.1 Ba. As a mineralogist, Tyler was pretty sure these particles were not minerals, but lacking much of a biological or palaeontological background he could not be sure what kind of fossils they were; and, even if genuinely organic, were they the same age as the rocks? Perhaps they were some more recent contaminant?

Fortunately Tyler was directed towards Elso S. Barghoorn (1915–84), a Harvard palaeobotanist of Finnish extraction, who specialised in the study of fungae. Barghoorn immediately realised that Tyler was onto something very new and potentially very big. Within a few months they fleshed out a short paper that was published in *Science* in 1954. They recognised five different kinds of microfossils – two algae, two fungi and a flagellated protozoan – but did not mention that they were all associated with *Cryptozoon*-type mounds because of the controversy still surrounding their nature. Only one of their 'algae' has stood the test of time, a form related to the cyanobacteria, but it was a landmark discovery and alerted palaeontologists to the possibility of discovering life in the deepest geological recesses of the Precambrian.

At the same time, unknown to most of the English-speaking scientific world (which was firmly in the paranoid grip of the Cold War) a Russian scientist was making an independent breakthrough into Precambrian fossil life. Boris Timofeev (1916–82), of the Leningrad Institute of Precambrian Geochronology, had also discovered microscopic organisms in Precambrian strata from the Urals.

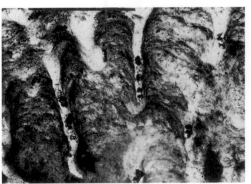

LEFT:
Circular microfossil-bearing, mound-shaped stromatolite structures in the Gunflint Chert beside Lake Superior, Canada, originally found by Stanley Tyler in 1953

BELOW:
A vertical slice through Gunflint Chert showing organic-rich laminae built up into branching mound structures called stromatolites (the bar is 1cm long)

Timofeev was searching the rocks in a more methodical way, using standard chemical techniques for the extraction of microfossils. He needed to search through greater volumes of rock and bulk samples were processed using appropriate acids, some of which are particularly dangerous, notably hydrofluoric acid (the only acid that can dissolve the quartz and other minerals of mudrocks and sandstones). Dissolving away the inorganic minerals of sediments leaves behind any organic matter as a black sludgy residue that often requires further drastic chemical treatment. More often than not there are no organics left and the Russians soon learned which kind of sediments were worth treating: dark-coloured shales and siltstones.

From the 1950s to 1970s Timofeev and his colleagues published a number of papers describing their finds of spore-like microfossils, but their important work gained virtually no international recognition because it was published in Russian journals that were not read in the West.

The Gunflint story really made news in 1965 when a detailed description by Tyler and Barghoorn appeared in *Science*. Tyler had died and Barghoorn and his student, J. William Schopf, had to pick up the pieces of unfinished manuscript. Even then publication had been spurred mainly by the

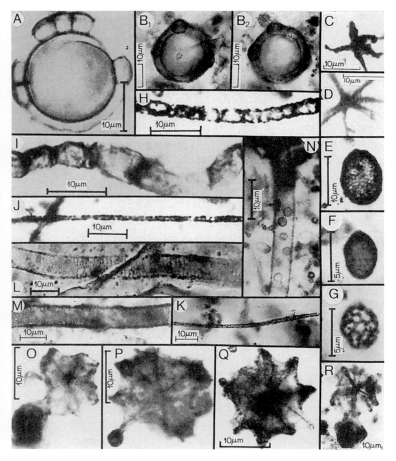

Labels within the figure: A, B₁, B₂, C, D, E, F, G, H, I, J, K, L, M, N, O, P, Q, R, with scale bars marked 10μm and 5μm.

ABOVE:
Details of microfossils within the Gunflint Chert from Canada, described by Elso Barghoorn, a Harvard palaeobotanist, and Stanley Tyler in 1954

threat of being gazumped by a rival, Preston Cloud (1912–91), who had searched out the lakeside locality and had been working away on the same fossil material independently. Barghoorn had been alerted to Cloud's pending publication and had beavered away to get his paper with the late Tyler out. First, he had to get Cloud to agree that he, Barghoorn, had priority in the matter.

Cloud's paper appeared a few weeks after the Tyler–Barghoorn one and, together, they hit the headlines around the world and received quite a lot of 'flak' from critics, who still doubted the authenticity of such ancient microfossils. Luckily Barghoorn had already been introduced to a new discovery from near Alice Springs in mid Australia. Again, some chert beds were associated with laminated *Cryptozoon*-like structures within the 850 Ma Precambrian Bitter Springs Formation strata. The discovery revealed hoards of microfossils with many new forms of spheres, filaments and clusters of cells, which were better preserved than the Gunflint fossils and closely resembled those of living

cyanobacteria. Precambrian palaeomicrobiology had taken off, and has never looked back.

One thing that the remarkable discoveries of soft-bodied microbes within very ancient strata should have taught us is not to be surprised at the continuing ability of the fossil record to open new windows into the past. One of the most remarkable of these recent windows gives us an astonishing view on the embryological development of some marine multi-celled invertebrates living in late Precambrian times. These microscopic clusters of developing cells were miraculously fossilised by mineral phosphate within hours of their fertilisation.

Embryos in apatite – 570 million years old

The fossil record normally just preserves the hard parts of organisms – the shells, teeth, bones and wood – whose material is robust enough to survive being pushed around by wind or water, buried in sediment and then survive processing within the Earth's crust before reappearing as petrified remains within rock strata. Soft body tissues are not normally preserved after being through the geological 'mill'. Consequently, most soft-bodied organisms are under-represented in the fossil record and many are not found at all, especially those that are small. This means that there is no fossil record of the early embryonic stages of life, when all multicelled organisms consist of incredibly small balls of dividing cells. At least, this was so until a decade or so ago.

In the 1980s Chinese scientists discovered some miracles of fossil preservation – microscopic embryonic spheres (less than 750 microns in diameter), around 570 million years old, buried in rock strata in southern China. To the astonishment of the scientific world, these minute mineralised balls were described (in 1998) as the fossilised embryos of primitive animals and plants. Not only that, but they present supporting palaeontological evidence for the divergence of animal phyla in the 'deep' Precambrian past, long before the start of the main fossil record at the beginning of Cambrian times, around 545

Rock of ages – dating rocks and fossils | **121**

Ma. The Chinese fossil embryos were one of the most exciting palaeontological finds of the last decades of the 20th century. They open a 'window' on a phase in the history of life that is very poorly represented by fossils, and show the enormous potential for soft tissue preservation that exists with certain kinds of fossilisation processes.

There is absolutely no doubt that these are genuine embryos, fossilised in the very early stages of cell division (cleavage) following fertilisation. Electron microscope images of the fossils show clusters of cells from the first two-cell division through to 'blackberry-like' spheres and cube-shaped packages of cells. They are all beautifully preserved in phosphatic minerals. Their form is identical to the different stages in cell division of living organisms. It appears that within hours of being shed into the sea by their parents, these eggs were fertilised, killed and preserved so well that they have survived for 570 million years.

Normally the soft cell material is not preserved by fossilisation but in exceptional conditions tough tissue, such as muscle and skin, may resist putrefaction long enough to be dehydrated or coated by bacterially released minerals and thus replicated and preserved. But most cell material is so 'watery' (over 98% water) and the bounding cell membrane so delicate that it normally ruptures within hours of death and is destroyed. With these embryos, the

process of fossilisation must have been extremely rapid with entombment in anoxic, phosphate-rich seawater and mud that was full of bacteria.

The seabed sediment/water interface and the top few centimetres of sediment are often highly charged with bacteria, and this is especially the case where there is little bottom-current activity, fine-grained sediment and oxygen depletion. Anaerobic bacteria thrive in such circumstances, becoming so abundant that they alter the local chemistry of the sediment. Such chemical changes can lead to the precipitation of various minerals such as pyrite (iron sulphide) and, in the Doushanto environment, phosphate mineral (calcium phosphate) coatings to the cells before the cell membranes broke down.

Unfortunately the patterns of early cell division in embryos are not particularly diagnostic for individual groups of animals. Physical constraints on tiny fluid-filled spheres and their close packing result in relatively few geometrical options. The cells behave rather like soap bubbles and take up honeycomb-like shapes and cluster just like blackberries. However, some configurations of these fossil embryos can be identified as typical of algae and sponges, and the latter is confirmed by the presence of sponge spicules. More important are those embryos that are characteristic of flatworms, nematodes and arthropods. This group of invertebrate animals is particularly

LEFT:
Modern stromatolites growing in Shark Bay, Western Australia (left) compared with similar 2,300-million-year-old mound-like structures in South Africa

interesting because they are multicellular organisms (metazoans) with a more advanced structure than sponges or algae. If the identification is correct, it provides supporting evidence that metazoans evolved well before 570 Ma and are just not well represented in the fossil record of late Precambrian times.

The molecular clock

The discovery and identification of the Doushanto embryos lends support to an estimate for the timing of metazoan evolution as suggested by the so-called 'molecular clock'. This clock is calibrated to an estimated standard rate of genetic change. By measuring the genetic 'distance' (comparison of gene sequences) between groups of living organisms, the time of original divergence can be calculated for a particular estimate of rate of genetic change. Recent attempts to do this have produced divergence dates for the metazoans as far back as 1.2 Ba. But other modifications of the method suggest a more reasonable and more generally accepted figure of 670 million years, and the Chinese embryos seem to support this more conservative estimate. The unique role of phosphate in the preservation and fossilisation of soft tissue is now much better understood and appreciated by palaeontologists, who are actively prospecting for other sedimentary phosphate deposits that might provide similarly preserved and privileged windows on the past. Some important sites of phosphate preservation have already been found, such as the late Cambrian *Orsten* strata of Sweden, which almost perfectly preserve in three-dimensions a variety of extinct small marine arthropods and the early Cretaceous Santana formation strata of Brazil, which preserves phosphatised gill and muscle tissues of fish. The further potential of this kind of preservation is enormous both within the Precambrian and younger Phanerozoic strata.

The surprising ability of the processes of fossilisation to occasionally preserve soft tissue has more direct implications for human history as it has allowed us to see something of the deep roots of the human 'family tree', which extend much further back in geological time than most people realise. By human 'family' I do not mean in the taxonomic sense, for the Family Hominidae to which we belong only includes members of the genus *Homo* and extends back just over 2 million years. Here I mean 'family' in the widest possible sense – all backboned animals (vertebrates) – which in taxonomic terms includes all mammals, birds, reptiles, amphibians, fish and their extinct fossil relatives.

RIGHT:

A reconstruction of the Earth 3,500 million years ago, with stromatolite mounds growing in shallow coastal waters of the early oceans, designed by K.M. Towe of the Smithsonian Institution in Washington, DC

Chapter 7

The 'deep' roots of the human family tree

Putting the backbone in life 530 million years ago

For most of the 19th century, the roots of the vertebrate 'family tree' were thought to lie buried way back in Silurian times, when fish-like backboned animals first appeared in the fossil record. It still is true that these strange-looking armoured and jawless fish first become common as fossils in Silurian age rocks. Their petrified remains are best known from marine strata in the Baltic and in Scotland. However, in recent decades, further rare and much older finds have been made in mid Ordovician sediments (470 Ma) from Bolivia in South America and in late Ordovician rocks from Australia and North America. There are also questionable bits and pieces from late Cambrian strata.

More importantly, two other recent developments have revolutionised our understanding of the vertebrate 'family tree'. One is the realisation that the extinct conodonts are significant 'players' in the story, and the other is the discovery of fossil chordates right back in early Cambrian age strata.

Biological understanding of our origin as backboned animals (vertebrates) is largely based on living animals. There is still a range of primitive vertebrate animals and their precursors, the chordates, alive today. We can see from developmental studies that the vertebrate backbone originated as an elongate, stiff but flexible rod, called the notochord, which runs along the back from the head to the tip of the tail in chordate animals such as the lancelet. The notochord can be flexed from side to side to produce a sinuous swimming motion by waves of contraction of muscle blocks on either side of the body. In the fish and all subsequent vertebrates like ourselves, the notochord has evolved into backbone (vertebral column). The cartilagineous or bony vertebrate backbone, with its articulating sections (vertebrae), strengthens the body, allowing it to grow to a considerable size (nearly 30m/98½ft in some dinosaurs and whales), support strut-like limbs and the heavy guts of large land-living plant eaters, protect the vital dorsal nerve cord and yet allow the body to flex.

The living primitive chordate, the lancelet *Branchiostoma*, is a curious little sea-dwelling, filter-feeding animal (about 5cm/2in long) that burrows tail-first into soft sand so that just its 'head' protrudes above the seabed. Its anterior end has little that distinguishes it; there is no separate head, no eyes or other well-developed sense organs, although there are some photoreceptor cells that might represent a precursor to the vertebrate eye. There is only a slight anterior swelling of the nerve cord, which can hardly be considered a 'brain'. Seawater is sucked through the mouth by a filter pump and its flow is maintained by beating cilia arranged along a series of slanting slotted bars. The water,

TERTIARY SYSTEM

CHALK SYSTEM.

OOLITE AND LIAS SYSTEMS

NEW RED SANDSTONE

CARBONIFEROUS SYSTEM

OLD RED SANDSTONE

SILURIAN SYSTEM.

Drawn & Engraved.   by John Emslie.

ABOVE:
One of the earliest time-lines (1849) for the history of life drawn by John Emslie and showing life beginning in Silurian times

plus food particles and dissolved oxygen, is sieved to remove 'rubbish' by a bunch of tentacles around the mouth. It then circulates through the pharynx, past the ciliated bars to remove food and oxygen, before passing back out of the body through a single opening. There is a simple gut leading to an anus, beyond which the body continues as a muscular tail. There is a simple circulatory system with open vessels, no heart and colourless blood.

Altogether, the lancelet has seemed to be a pretty simple animal and a long way from the most primitive fish, let alone any other vertebrates. However, recent research on its biology is showing up more and more details that reveal it to be more closely comparable to the basic vertebrate condition than previously suspected. The critical feature that differentiates the

The 'deep' roots of the human family tree |

chordates from the vertebrates is seen in the development of the neural crest cells within the embryo. In the vertebrates some of these cells break away to form structures such as the eyes, skull support structures (skull) and head muscles. Although the lancelet does not have a true neural crest, it does have cells in a similar position that express similar genes.

So the lancelet does provide a very interesting model of what the earliest chordates might have been like. However, when the biology of the lancelet first became well known, there seemed to be little hope that the fossil record would be of much help in revealing anything about the lancelet's ancestry because these chordates have no skeletal hard parts which can be preserved under normal processes of fossilisation. Nevertheless, against all expectations and Darwin's gloomy predictions about the uselessness of the fossil record in supporting the theory of evolution, there have been some rare circumstances of preservation have confounded the pessimists.

Pikaia opens a can of 'worms'

In the latter part of the 1960s, a couple of small quarries high up in the Canadian Rockies were reopened and worked purely for their fossils and research interest, as they had been in the early decades of the century. The fossils came from the Burgess Shale, a mid-Cambrian deposit of seabed muds, originally excavated by Charles Doolittle Walcott, several of whose discoveries have contributed to our story of petrified life. The outstanding importance of the Burgess Shale fossils lies in the preservation of their soft tissues, revealing new anatomical details of these ancient life forms and many entirely new fossil organisms with no hard parts at all, including an astonishing diversity of 'worms' and arthropods.

Walcott opens a window on life 520 million years ago

The 1909 'accidental' discovery of fossils high on a mountainside in the Canadian Rockies, by Walcott, opened one of the world's most famous 'windows' into the deep past. The fossiliferous strata, called the Burgess Shale and now known to be some 520 million years old, have yielded tens of thousands of remarkable fossils, many of which still have some of their soft parts petrified and preserved by minerals. These early Cambrian age fossils range from entirely soft-bodied worms, sponges and chordates to a vast diversity of arthropods with their legs and other appendages and sometimes even their guts preserved. Altogether they illuminate a clear view of life in early Cambrian seas when arthropods first came to power and our most remote vertebrate ancestors were just tiny lamprey-like creatures a few centimetres in size. The mountainside locality is now a protected World Heritage Site within British Columbia's Yoho National Park.

Discovering the Burgess Shale

In 1844 a surveyor building the railway link through the spectacular Kicking Horse Valley in the Rocky Mountains of western Canada first discovered trilobite fossils on the steep flanks of Mount Stephen. However, the Burgess Shale and its particular fossil fauna was not found until 31 August 1909 when Walcott, accompanied by his wife and son, chanced upon it as they made their way across the high ridge connecting Mount Field and Wapta Mountain.

Walcott spotted a profusion of fossils in a scree block of hard shale and immediately recognised their potential importance. Not only were the usual hard parts of the fossils preserved but also soft tissues, such as delicate appendages. Over the next eight years Walcott systematically quarried into the mountainside and excavated some 70,000 specimens from the Burgess Shale 'mother lode' and shipped them back to the Smithsonian Institution in Washington DC. Over the succeeding years he described over 100 new species from the Burgess Shale, but this was only the tip of the taxonomic 'iceberg'. Because of administrative duties, he had little opportunity to research the full significance of his find.

Walcott has been variously described as 'a good man' and 'an important unknown figure'. His is a typical American success

ABOVE:

Walcott directing excavations of the mid Cambrian age Burgess Shale in the Canadian Rockies, from which over 70,000 fossils, mostly arthropods, have been recovered

story. With little formal education (not even completing high school), he nevertheless rose to become director of the US Geological Survey (from 1894), then Secretary of the Smithsonian Institution (1907–27) and President of the National Academy of Sciences (1917–23), one of the most powerful organisations of science in the world. Such an ascent would be virtually impossible today with our premium on paper qualifications.

For the majority of people who are even familiar with his name, Walcott is probably just a footnote, 'the guy who stumbled across the Burgess Shale by accident in 1909'. Only specialist palaeontologists are familiar with his published work on Cambrian stratigraphy, arthropods and the trilobites in particular. In fact, Walcott's collected works run to over five volumes and range well beyond the Burgess fossils. Walcott saw that he could be of more 'use' to the scientific community as a right-minded and committed public servant than a narrowly focused research palaeontologist. So because of official duties

Walcott's priorities had to be redirected, away from his beloved trilobite and other fossils, and towards the larger goal of American geology and science in general. His private journals are full of recurring plaintive entries about 'odd moments spent with Cambrian brachiopods'. But Walcott was lucky to live at a time when, geologically, North America was still very much unexplored territory.

Cambrian sea world

The astonishing diversity of Burgess Shale life was more fully revealed in the late 1960s, largely through the work of a British palaeontologist Harry Whittington and his research students in the University of Cambridge. More recently the Geological Survey of Canada has reworked some of the quarries and opened new ones, providing another fossil bonanza, which has helped resolve many of the outstanding palaeontological problems arising from the difficulty of assigning some of the Burgess organisms to known fossil groups.

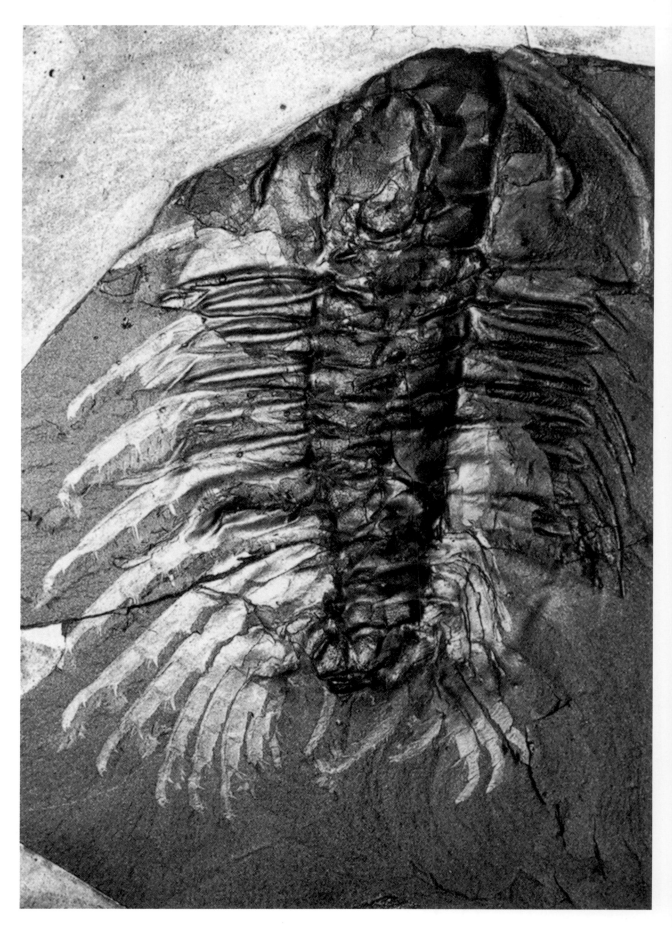

OPPOSITE:
Olenoides, *a trilobite
from the Burgess Shale
with soft tissues such as
its legs preserved in the
very fine marine mud
rock*

These detailed investigations show that, however measured, the Burgess sea world was dominated by an extraordinary diversity of arthropods which comprise around 50% of all the Burgess Shale individuals, species and biomass. It has been calculated that in biomass terms sponges, echinoderms and priapulid worms were around 10% each, so that together with the trilobites these groups of animals account for some 80% of the total biomass. A less conspicuous inhabitant was a curious swimming creature *Pikaia*, which may be a remote ancestor of all vertebrates – including ourselves.

The 20 or so different fossil arthropods, one of the first groups of animals to have well-developed eyes, range across many different lifestyles. The trilobite *Olenoides* crawled around on the seabed and ate organic detritus; the strange *Anomalocaris*, the most awesome of the Burgess creatures, was a free-swimming predator and the largest animal of its time, growing to around 60cm (23½in) in length. For over 100 years it was only known from fragmentary remains and these were thought to belong to three quite different animals. The disc-like mouth was seen as a jellyfish, the long front limbs as the tail of a shrimp-like arthropod and part of the body as a sponge. Finally, in 1985, British palaeontologists Harry Whittington and Derek Briggs saw the light and reassembled the bits as one animal – *Anomalocaris* – 'unusual shrimp'.

Numerous sponges grew up from the seabed and provided anchorage for bivalve-shelled brachiopods along with stalked echinoderm sealilies and an Ediacaran survivor, the seapen *Thaumaptilon*. A variety of worms hid in the sediment, including a toothed priapulid, the voracious predator *Ottoia*. The mollusc-like *Wiwaxia* ploughed across the mud surface. Its protective scaly armour shows what some of the early Cambrian scale-bearing animals looked like. There were spectacularly 'hairy', surface-living polychaete worms, such as *Canadia* and *Burgessochaeta*, bristling with thousands of tiny hair-like chaetae.

These bristles and many of the finely ridged scales and plates of the Burgess animals are thought to have acted as diffraction gratings for display lighting. In the dim bluish light, filtering down from the sea surface, the gratings and hairs would have flashed silver and grey colours as the animals moved, allowing them to recognise one another. The problem is that they would have become equally conspicuous to the newly evolved predators but their 'armour' of bristles and plates would also have served to protect them.

Overall the division of 'labour' between the Burgess organisms is similar to that found in modern marine ecosystems. Recognition of this remarkable diversity and level of ecological sophistication so early in animal evolution has led scientists to doubt older claims that there was an 'explosive' radiation of life at the base of the Cambrian. They now speculate that there must have been a lengthy earlier development of vertebrate and more especially invertebrate life stretching back into Precambrian times, perhaps as far as 850 million years ago.

BELOW:
Canadia, *a Burgess
Shale marine polychaete
worm with its delicate
bristles, which may
originally have been
iridescent, preserved*

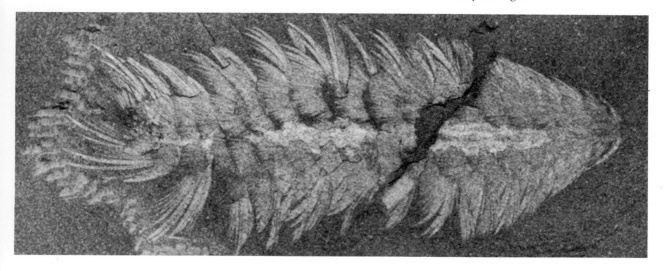

Preservation

Because the Burgess Shale has been caught up in the formation of the Rocky Mountains, the mudrocks have suffered considerable compression and some heating. It is somewhat surprising that soft tissues are preserved because the fossils have been severely flattened and it is extremely difficult to reconstruct their original 3D form.

The main reason that so many organisms are so well preserved is the result of a catastrophic event. Originally the organisms lived in and around gently shelving soft seabed muds at a depth of some 70m (230ft). An earthquake caused the mud to suddenly liquidise and cascade downslope as a submarine avalanche, carrying away everything living on or in the mud. When the flow was arrested, the creatures were entombed within the sticky mud. Their bad luck was science's good fortune. By meticulous research and analysis of the contorted bodies of the inhabitants of the 520 Ma Burgess Shale, a privileged window has been opened on the life of Middle Cambrian times.

Burgess Shale-like faunas have now been found from Cambrian rocks elsewhere in the world from Greenland to China. However, the fossils coming out of these deposits continue to fascinate and puzzle palaeontologists. The richest of the new finds is that of Chenjiang in China which, being Lower Cambrian in age, is slightly older than the Burgess Shale and has the additional benefit of not being slightly metamorphosed and deformed. As a result the anatomy and biology of some of the more problematic rare and often fragmentary Burgess animals is being resolved. No longer can the Burgess Shale be described as a collection of evolutionary one-offs with 'no place to go' within the taxonomy of living animals.

One of the thousands of fossils found by Walcott over the years was a little (4cm/1½in-long) sliver of a thing, which he called *Pikaia gracilens*, meaning the 'slim and elegant' fossil from Pika, a mountain near the quarries in British Columbia. Walcott described the flattened, ribbon-shaped and clearly segmented creature as a polychaete worm, and little attention was paid to it for another 50 years.

In the 1960s English palaeontologist Harry Whittington was a professor in Harvard and was invited by the Geological Survey of Canada to reopen the Burgess Shale quarries. This eventually happened in 1966-7 and huge quantities of new fossils were obtained. Whittington had by this time been moved back to England to take up the prestigious and historic Woodwardian chair of palaeontology in the University of Cambridge. Over the succeeding decades he parcelled out the Burgess fossils to a succession of research students, and the 'worms' went to Simon Conway Morris. By this time it had become apparent that there was perhaps more to *Pikaia* than Walcott thought.

Although all the details are still not published, Conway Morris has shown that this tiny, lancelet-shaped and sized creature shares several important features with the living lancelet. It too lacks a well-defined head but clearly show traces of an elongate notochord, dorsal nerve cord and paired blocks of muscles down either side of the body – all those critical chordate features for the evolution of backboned animals.

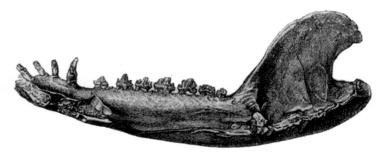

ABOVE:
The first early fossil mammal to be discovered in the 1820s was this marsupial-like triconodont jawbone of Jurassic age from Stonesfield in Oxfordshire, called Phascolotherium *by Buckland*

However, there are some important differences, such as the apparent lack of an extension of the notochord into the anteriormost part of the animal and the presence of a pair of lobes with long tentacles in the 'head' region. Nevertheless, palaeobiologists such as Simon Conway Morris are satisfied that *Pikaia* is a lancelet-like primitive chordate.

As such it was seen to confirm the extended ancestry of the chordates and probably the vertebrates back into Cambrian times some 520 million years ago. But *Pikaia*'s hegemony as one of our earliest ancestors was relatively short-lived. By the 1990s a new and slightly older array of spectacular fossils from lower Cambrian age strata in China was hitting the headlines. Like the Burgess fossils, those of the Chenjiang deposit preserve soft tissues, but the Chinese ones are somewhat better preserved and easier to prepare than those of the Burgess.

Chinese ancestors

Again, some curious little lancelet-like fossils turned up amongst an amazing array of arthropods and worms of all kinds. *Yunnanozoon* was the first to be described in 1995 and was soon followed by three others, one of which, *Haikouella*, is represented by over 300 specimens. Unlike *Yunnanozoon* and *Pikaia*, *Haikouella* seems to have a distinct but simple heart, dorsal and ventral aortic blood vessels, gill filaments, a more distinct head with forward swelling of the dorsal nerve cord (primitive brain?), possible eyes and perhaps some pharyngeal teeth. If all these features can be confirmed, then this creature represents a considerable advance on the lancelet-like condition seen in *Pikaia* and, interestingly, it is older.

Around the same time another Chinese team, in collaboration with Simon Conway Morris, found and described two more new chordates from the Chenjiang. In addition to the features seen in *Haikouella*, they seem to preserve a skull-like structure, presumably made originally of cartilage along with gill arches, fin supports, better defined eye capsules and a large heart behind the gills. This combination would seem to place these animals *Myllokunmingia* (the fish from Kunming) and *Haikouichthys* (the fish from Haikou) as primitive vertebrates. All this new evidence would seem to suggest that vertebrates initially arose as actively swimming animals, with well-developed sensory apparatus (eyes and perhaps chemoreceptors), coordinated by a developing anterior brain, which was supported and protected by a non-mineralised 'brain-box/skull'. The later Cambrian to end Triassic conodont animals perhaps represent the first vertebrates with mineralised tissues, not in the form of skeletal tissue but teeth allied to a predatory habit.

Furthermore, the researchers claim that *Myllokunmingia* is closer to the living jawless hagfish and *Haikouichthys* to the living jawless lampreys. If this true, it would indicate that these two vertebrate groups had already split by early Cambrian times and must have shared a common ancestor in an even earlier epoch, presumably within the late Precambrian. Such an early ancestry is supported by molecular clock evidence derived from measures of the genetic distance between living lancelets, the hagfish and lampreys, which dates a common vertebrate ancestry at around 750 million years ago.

The evolutionary significance of the conodonts is considerable. They demonstrate that the vertebrate mineralised skeleton may have evolved as an adaptation for more successful raptorial feeding. If so, the conodont promotion of the vertebrate arms race turns conventional wisdom on its head. It was previously thought that the vertebrate mineralised skeleton, in the form of the dermal armour of the extinct jawless fish, had evolved as a form of protection against predators.

The other end of the human 'family tree', in the widest sense, concerns those warm-blooded, hairy beasts like ourselves that we know as the mammals (Class Mammalia). Surprisingly, perhaps, more publicity has been given to fossil dinosaurs than to our own mammalian ancestors, although when our early mammalian evolution is detailed it does become clear why this is so. Our mammalian ancestors were far from the mythical, dragon-like monsters whose iconic status has been displaced by the dinosaurs; they were closer to the 'tim'rous beasties' celebrated by the Scottish poet Robert Burns (1759–96). But we do have something of a vested interest in their early evolutionary history, even if they were all rather unimpressive shrew-sized beasts.

Finding the first mammals

Fossils of early mammals were first discovered as long ago as the mid 19th century within Triassic strata in Germany. Two small teeth, found near Stuttgart in 1847, were seen to have the distinctive complex pattern of cusps and hollows that distinguish mammalian cheek teeth (molars) and were named as *Microlestes*, meaning 'small predator'. The existence of mammal fossils as far back as Jurassic times had been proven at the beginning of the 19th century by the discovery of lower jawbones from three different kinds of mole-sized mammals found in the Stonesfield oolite limestones of Oxfordshire, the same rock strata that had provided the first dinosaur fossils.

Although biologically important, the discovery of these mammal fossils and any publicity associated with them was largely eclipsed by greater interest in the much more exotic extinct reptiles. The small size of the mammal fossils contributed to their lack of allure. Subsequent discoveries of early mammals have verified the fact that the first mammals were all small shrew-to-hedgehog-sized creatures. As such they had good reason to be like the poet, Robert Burns's, 'wee, sleekit, cow'rin, tim'rous beastie', full of 'panic in thy breastie', and would need to be able to 'start awa sae hasty', considering the company they kept. Their world was populated by an enormous diversity of reptiles, not only dinosaurs of all sizes.

As we have seen, Cuvier examined them on a visit to Oxford's Ashmolean Museum in 1818. He thought that they belonged to marsupial mammals, but noted that they differed from living marsupials and all known mammals in having 10 molar cheek teeth. One of the specimens was illustrated and described as a fossil marsupial, *Thylacotherium*, by the French palaeontologist Constant Prevost in 1825. Richard Owen pointed out that the jawbone must belong to an extinct genus because of the number of molars. He also claimed that it might have an affinity with the newly discovered numbat, a squirrel-shaped, termite-eating marsupial technically known as *Myrmecobius*, which was first found in a hollow tree, surrounded by anthills, near the Swan River in south-east Australia. This was a great period of biological discovery, with new animals and plants being found all over the globe and brought back to fill the new natural history museums of the great metropolitan centres of the Western world.

When another, better preserved, fossil jaw was found at Stonesfield, Richard Owen was able to show that *Thylacotherium* was not a marsupial but a placental insectivore. He renamed it *Amphitherium* in 1846, although it does preserve some features similar to the marsupials. The other Stonesfield specimen, *Phascolotherium*, seemed to him to be a genuine marsupial.

Charles Lyell, in 1853, was so impressed by the occurrence of 'these most ancient memorials of the mammiferous type... in so low a member of the oolitic series. (They)

should serve as a warning to us against hasty generalisations, founded solely on negative evidence...' He eventually gets to the point: 'It seems fatal to the theory of progressive development, or to the notion that the order of precedence in the creation of animals, considered chronologically, has precisely coincided with the order in which they would be ranked according to perfection or complexity of structure'. Remember that this was *before* the Darwin/Wallace theory of evolution, and Lyell was arguing against any idea of progressive development. He thought that the fossil record of most groups of animals and plants would eventually be found to extend back to some common starting point (act of Creation) in the Transition strata, which were later named as Cambrian by Adam Sedgwick.

Identifying fossil mammals

Our own class of backboned animals, the mammals, has some key characters that separate us from the reptiles and other vertebrates. Mammals are warm-blooded, covered in hair and give birth to live young that are suckled by milk, secreted from the mother's mammary glands. However, the discovery of the egg-laying monotremes showed that distinction of the mammals, as a watertight group might not be quite so leakproof. Consequently there has been an ongoing argument about how the mammal/non-mammal boundary should be defined and where it should be placed in relation to the placental mammals (those, like most mammals, with a long gestation in the womb), marsupial mammals, monotremes and other extinct fossil groups, such as the multituberculates. So the straightforward question of the age of the oldest mammal cannot be answered without asking the question – what is meant by mammal?

Any appeal for help from the fossil record is complicated by the problematic nature of the fossil remains of mammals. The problem for the palaeontologist is that none of the key traits, which are linked to soft tissues, is generally preserved in a fossil record that is mostly comprised of bones and teeth. Fortunately there are some skeletal features associated with being a mammal as opposed to a reptile. Mammals have highly specialised teeth, a lower jawbone made of a single bony element, called the dentary, and three small middle-ear bones. In contrast, reptiles can be distinguished by their relatively simple and similar teeth. They also have a lower jaw comprised of more than one bony element, and a single middle-ear bone. As mammals evolved from reptiles, bones from the lower jaw have been modified to form those of the middle ear.

All living mammals, including the monotremes, share a synapsid skull form (which has a single pair of openings low down in the skull behind the eyes) with some reptiles. Detailed assessment of the biology of the living synapsid mammals shows that the monotremes and therian mammals (those that give birth to live young – marsupials and placentals) diverged from a common ancestor. It is therefore probably most expedient to confine the class of mammals to these groups. Since the fossil record has thrown up a number of extinct mammal-like animals, whose reproductive biology is not directly known, they are best regarded as mammaliaforms. One of the most remarkable of these is the recently found 195-million-year-old *Hadrocodium* from the early Jurassic Lufeng deposits of Yunnan Province, China.

Miniscule mammal

With a skull just 12mm (½in) long and an estimated body weight of 2g (0.07oz), *Hadrocodium* might be miniscule but it has an importance that is quite disproportionate to its fingernail size. *Hadrocodium*, one of the smallest of all mammals – extant or extinct – is described by a Sino–American team led by Zhe-Xi Luo as belonging to an extinct group of mammal-like animals that evolved before the common ancestors of the true mammals. Although so small, the skull is exceptionally well preserved in three dimensions and shows a number of adult features, such as the presence of a large diastema or gap behind the canine teeth and wear on its molar teeth, that prove that the animal had developed beyond an early juvenile stage.

From our perspective it might be an evolutionary sideshow, but it has features that are forcing a revision of ideas about when the essential mammal characters first appeared. Surprisingly, the tiny *Hadrocodium* skull still preserves its even smaller ear bones. More surprisingly still, it has already evolved to a stage where there are three middle-ear bones and, in one fell swoop, extends the first known appearance of this critical feature back in time by some 45 million years. As a result, it has a single jawbone (dentary) plus other features, such as an advanced form of secondary palate, which separates the mouth from the nasal passage, and an enlarged brain cavity.

Altogether these features show that there was considerable evolutionary variability within the different groups of early mammals. The diagnostic characters for the living mammals appear in a stepwise and incremental fashion to produce an additive pattern over some 100 million years within the evolution of extinct mammaliaforms. According to Zhe-Xi Luo and colleagues, 'There was no single episode of rapid evolution'.

Such variation so early in these mammaliaforms reinforces the view that early mammal evolution extends well back into Triassic times. The Mesozoic era might be known as the 'Age of Reptiles', but in many ways the days of the big reptiles were already numbered, as soon as they began. Equally, the following Cenozoic 'Age of Mammals' might also be just as numbered and there might be some group of small animals waiting in the wings for their turn on the evolutionary stage – the rodents perhaps, or maybe the birds?

The body mass of *Hadrocodium* is estimated from its skull size, using a well-established scaling relationship based on 64 living insectivore mammals, of which the smallest weighs 2.5g (0.09oz). By comparison, the smallest bat has a similar weight to *Hadrocodium*, which is the smallest known Mesozoic mammal whose overall weight range extends from 3–517g (0.1g–18oz). The fossil record shows that this weight range had already been achieved by the early Jurassic Lufeng mammals, and that a considerable ecological diversity had already been established.

Dawn mother

The year 2002 saw the arrival of yet another stunning fossil from China. Appropriately named *Eomaia scansoria* ('dawn mother'), it is an almost perfectly preserved skeleton of a mouse-sized mammal. Amazingly, 125 million years after the animal died, it is still covered in fossilised hair, one of those soft-tissue features unique to the mammals. Already the hair seems to be differentiated into a dense layer of underhair, covered with sparser and longer guard hairs and capable of acting as an efficient insulator. Although the skeleton is inevitably flattened, as these early Cretaceous lakeshore muds were compressed into rock, it preserves most of the bones, including millimetre-sized foot bones, claws, cartilages and teeth.

Most importantly, detailed examination of the remains by Qiang Ji and his collaborators from Beijing and the Carnegie Museum of Natural History shows that *Eomaia* is by far the oldest known representative of the Eutheria (the placental mammals). It is thus separate from the primitive egg-laying and pouched mammals such as the duck-billed platypus and kangaroo. Because its pelvic outlet is so narrow, *Eomaia* probably gave birth to immature young. They would have required nutrition from their mother, and protection within a marsupial-like pouch. If this interpretation is correct, then *Eomaia* is one of the most primitive eutherians known.

Examination of the limb bones shows that it has long finger and toe bones with strongly curved and sideways, flattened claws, all features similar to those of the living dormice which feed and nest above ground and are specialised for climbing. *Eomaia* had an estimated body mass of 20–25g (0.7–0.88oz), again similar to that of the smallest dormice species. There is speculation that the ability to climb was part of the early evolutionary success of the eutherians. However, since the fossil record of mammals is primarily made up of teeth and bits of jawbone, it is not until 50 million years later that the next eutherian fossil skeletons appear in the fossil record. By this time they had diversified to include forms that were specialised for running and hopping. The problem is that the fossil

record shows that the earliest true marsupials were also climbers, which suggests that the common ancestor of both groups was also a climber. Given the competition from the ruling reptiles of the time, it is likely that the best option for these small primitive mammals was to escape into the trees or underground and only to be active at night.

Eomaia is not the only mammal fossil to be found in the Yixian Formation strata of Liaoning Province in north-eastern China, but it is the most spectacular. Three other mammal relatives have been found in the last decade. *Jeholodens, Repenomanus* and *Zhangheotherium* are members of other primitive mammal lineages that have not survived to the present day. This early diversity shows, yet again, that evolution is often very shrubby, with several innovatory groups arising from a common stem. Since they all had teeth suggestive of carnivorous and insectivorous diets, there may not have been much to differentiate between them at the time, except that they were of different sizes and probably exploited different ecological niches.

The biggest was *Repenomanus*, which, with its 11cm (4.3in) skull, probably was big enough to swallow *Eomaia* whole. At this size it must have been ground-dwelling, as was *Jeholodens*, the smallest of all; it has short fingers and toes, with broad claws, which would have been no good at gripping plant stems. Finally *Zhangheotherium*, with its short straight fingers but long curved claws, was slightly bigger than *Eomaia* and may well have also been a climber. Considering the diversity of reptilian predators that they lived amongst, these mammals must have been well adapted to have survived at all.

The Yixian Formation is one of the world's great fossil 'goldmines' and has, so far, provided us with the stunning fossils of feathered dinosaurs *Sinosauropteryx, Protarchaeopteryx* and *Caudipteryx*; primitive birds *Confuciusornis* and *Liaoningornis*; one of the oldest flowering plants, *Archaefructus*; as well as a host of other fossil plants, insects, clams, snails, fish, salamanders, turtles, lizards, a frog, and pterosaur *Eosipterus*.

BELOW:
Zhangotherium, a new and spectacularly well-preserved primitive rat-sized symmetrodont mammal, some 125 million years old, from the early Cretaceous deposits of north-east China

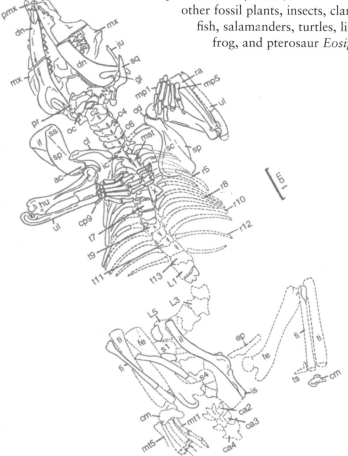

Chapter 8

Ancient DNA – fossilising a fragile molecule

The newest revolution to impact upon the study of fossils is the discovery and recovery of ancient biomolecules, especially ancient DNA. In conjunction with the mapping of the genome of an increasing number of organisms from yeast to the chick, mouse and now humans, DNA is helping to answer some evolutionary problems and raising many more. Genomic mapping of a wider range of plants and animals will give a new perspective on the evolution of life. Molecular 'clock' estimates of the timing of important evolutionary divergences will help test the completeness of the fossil record and the way that it biases our view of the past.

Ever since 1953, when Francis Crick and James Watson discovered the structure of DNA and effectively the mechanism by which cells are replicated, research into all aspects of DNA has boomed. We all – indeed, every organism – carry our own version of the DNA molecule around in every cell of our bodies. The discovery of how the genetic code for life is passed on from generation to generation has so many ramifications. Almost everyone is now familiar with the forensic use of DNA: how a speck of blood can be used to point a genetic 'finger' at a murderer. Almost as much publicity has been given to the *Jurassic Park* story and the idea of bringing the dinosaurs back to life through the recovery of fossil DNA. But the actual recovery has had a troubled and less

spectacular history.

The business of recovering and analysing DNA is a complex, highly technical and very time-consuming business, and is so sensitive that the process can be set off by a single molecule of DNA. Unless the analytical equipment is ultra-squeaky clean, it will amplify any old bit of DNA hanging around in the system – a bacterium or speck of dandruff from a technician will do.

Old DNA was first extracted in 1984 from the dried, museum-preserved skin of a quagga, a zebra-like animal from southern Africa that was hunted to extinction over a hundred years ago. The last quagga died in Amsterdam zoo in 1887. In the mid 1980s one of the first attempts to extract more ancient fossil biomolecules showed that albumen from a frozen 40,000-year-old baby mammoth differed from the albumen of living elephants by no more than about 1%. Such a small difference implied that mammoths and living elephants all shared a common ancestor around 5 million years ago. That result really started the molecular palaeontology race going, but initially it proved frustratingly difficult.

Nevertheless, the dedicated few persisted with the search for better and older material. Fossil DNA could show how evolution works in detail by revealing how genetic inheritance changes over time in successive generations of organisms. But to do this it is necessary to find a type of 'petrification' in which organisms were virtually buried alive. Ideally they have to be sealed in a capsule that dehydrates the body and provides an antiseptic environment excluding any microbes that would cause decay and leave confusing traces of their own DNA – a tall order for the natural environment.

The natural deep-freeze of the polar permafrost can preserve ancient tissues and biomolecules wonderfully well, but this kind of record only extends back a few tens of thousands of years. Some of the ancient DNA hunters seem to have been more concerned with another goal – scientific fame, its attendant public recognition and bigger research grants – for being the first to recover 'seriously' old DNA, and so the race began. The competing research teams pinned their hopes on the unique properties of fossil amber resin. For hundreds of years amber has been known to include small creatures, especially insects, in what seemed like perfect preservational circumstances. Amber seemed to promise a quality of petrification as near to the ideal as we can get, outside a deep-freeze.

The promise of amber

Amber has been coveted and endowed with special worth for time immemorial; amulets of amber have been found dating back as far as 35,000 years. In 1701 King Frederick I of Prussia commissioned an entire room made of amber as a gift for Peter the Great of Russia. Historically that probably represented the peak of value for amber. Since then our appreciation of it as a decorative material worth its weight in gold has declined, but only slightly. Amber has been in and out of fashion over the last century or so, experiencing something of a renaissance in Victorian times when amber beads adorned ample matronly bosoms. Even chunkier amber jewellery returned to

favour in Denmark, Germany and Britain in the latter decades of the 20th century. However, at the same time it took on a very different promise as a potential store of fossil DNA.

Scientific interest in amber has similarly fluctuated over the centuries. Embedded small organisms – commonly insects, but ranging from ferns to frogs and feathers – have always been part of amber's allure. In the 1st century AD Pliny the Elder noted that amber was the 'discharge of a pine-like tree, originated in the north and often contained small insects'. His compatriot Marcus Valerius Martialis was more poetic: 'The bee is enclosed, and shines preserved in amber, so that it seems enshrined in its own nectar'. It was not until the 19th century that the collection of amber flora and fauna really got under way.

The largest hoard was of Baltic origin, amassed by an innkeeper, Wilhelm Stantien, and a merchant, Moritz Becker. They used dredging and mining techniques to extract pieces of amber from the unconsolidated marine greensands and clays of Tertiary age (Eocene, 38 million years ago) in the Samland peninsula, near Kaliningrad on the Russian Baltic seaboard. The vast bulk of this material did not contain any fossil remains and was sold. But a huge collection of some 120,000 amber-embedded animal and plant fossils were recovered and housed in the Konigsberg University Geological Institute Museum. Unfortunately, despite being dispersed for safety during World War II, much of this amazing collection was lost, presumably destroyed or stolen.

Although the 'depth of view' of the insect life in Baltic forests of Eocene age is sadly no longer available in a single collection, we can still catch glimpses of it. There are large collections of Baltic amber in public museums around the world, but sadly in total they do not amount to much more than that one unrepeatable collection. The Natural History Museum in London has a 'mere' 25,000-odd specimens.

There are various popular misconceptions about amber: for example, that it is the fossilised resin of coniferous trees from the Baltic region and that its abundance is the result of some unusual condition of

RIGHT:
38 million year old (Eocene age) amber from the Baltic has long been famous for the fossil insects which are sometimes found embedded in it

these ancient trees. It is true that an astonishing amount of amber has been recovered from this region. Stantien and Becker's operations alone produced between a quarter and a half a million tons a year between 1875 and 1914, probably well over 10 million tons altogether.

However, modern research has debunked the myths about how amber was formed. The most likely arboreal candidate to have produced the Baltic amber is an araucariacean tree similar to the living *Agathis* from New Zealand. The araucariacean tree secretes copious preservable resin that could well accumulate to this order of magnitude, given the appropriate geological time scale of hundreds of thousands, if not millions, of years.

The Baltic region was only one of many, from the Dominican Republic, to China and Rumania, that produced amber in Tertiary times. Furthermore, amber-resin-producing trees are shown to have an extended geological history way back to Cretaceous times, over 100 million years ago, and possibly as far back as the Carboniferous (over 300 million years ago). Many of these older ambers have not been rigorously investigated with modern techniques and taxonomic know-how.

Detailed study of these ambers and their contained fossils is providing unique insights into life in the amber forests of the past. For many insects, such as the hairy fungus beetles (Mycetophagidae) or the flat-footed flies (Platypezidae), amber

provides the main source of their previous existence. As Swift wrote: 'So, naturalists observe, a flea/Has smaller fleas that on him prey;/And these have smaller still to bite 'em;/And so proceed ad infinitum'. We can see them all in amber, from the parasitic wasp larva on its spider host to the flies the spider trapped.

George Poinar, an American entomologist, headed a Californian research team (at Berkeley) and in 1982 first tried to realize the potential of Dominican amber for the extraction of fossil DNA when he described ultrastructural detail of body tissue within an amber-embedded fly. Poinar's work stimulated Michael Crichton's fertile imagination to create his 1990 sci-fi thriller *Jurassic Park*. It seemed a 'neat' idea at the time: Jurassic mosquito bites dinosaur, sucking out a sample of blood, then mosquito inadvertently lands on aromatic amber resin and becomes mired. The amber flows over the mosquito, trapping both mosquito DNA and the DNA in dinosaur blood cells. All the microbiologist has to do is find a sample of amber entombing a perfectly preserved mosquito, then extract and amplify the dinosaur DNA... and so on. However, there are a few technical snags with the idea, beginning with the lack of mosquitoes in Jurassic times, not to mention the paucity of Jurassic amber, most of which is Tertiary in age, by which time the dinosaurs were extinct.

However, it was an American East Coast team led by Rob DeSalle of the American Museum of Natural History in New York and colleagues who claimed, in 1992, to get the most interesting and detailed fossil DNA from a Tertiary fossil termite *Mastotermes electrodominicus* embedded in amber. Then another Pacific Coast team, led by Raul Cano of California Polytechnic State University, claimed to have extracted and amplified fragmentary DNA from a stingless bee, *Proplebeia dominicana*. Both insects came from the extraordinary fauna that has been found in Oligo–Miocene (Tertiary age) amber, presently being mined in considerable quantity in the Dominican Republic. The fauna is by no means restricted to insects and includes rarities like a frog, mushroom and mammalian

LEFT:
Scientific study of fossils embedded in amber shows that in Eocene *times northern Europe was much warmer than today and covered in subtropical forest*

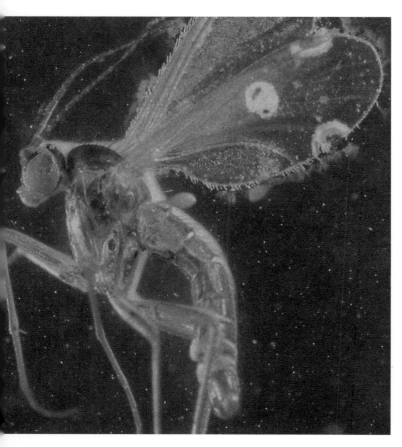

hair, so there seemed to be enormous scope for future exploration of these organic inclusions in amber.

In 1993 the Poinar team made a quantum leap back in time when they claimed to have obtained DNA from a 130-million-year-old (early Cretaceous) weevil. This seemed to push the possibility of extracting at least part of the 'code of life' back to the time, if not the actual life, of the dinosaurs. It seemed to be a case of the science catching up with the fiction it originally spawned, and specifically the *Jurassic Park* story. This was soon followed by further claims of fossil DNA being obtained directly from dinosaur fossils themselves, mainly bones. However, some fossil DNA specialists such as Svaante Pääbo were highly sceptical about the quality and validity of these results, especially as none of the results had been replicated by independent analysis in different labs.

In the late 1990s a new lab was set up in the Natural History Museum in London, dedicated to extraction and analysis of nothing else but DNA from amber-embedded specimens drawn from the

Museum's extensive collections. Every care was taken to maintain DNA 'hygiene' and there were runs of successive trials to replicate any positive results but unfortunately, there were no positive results. The team was forced to conclude that all previous claims of fossil DNA from amber was spurious contamination from the lab environment.

Despite this severe knock-back, more cautious researchers continued to get good results from much more recent material. They researched the postmortem conditions under which DNA is either destroyed or preserved, so that they could go out and actively prospect for those sites that would stand a better chance of retaining fragments of this very delicate molecule.

The search continues elsewhere

The complex organic molecules that comprise cellular material break down rapidly after death, unless preserved by rapid freezing or dehydration, processes that are rare in nature. It was soon realised that the best chances of DNA preservation require fossilisation in cool, dark situations such as caves for bones, or freeze-drying in permafrost, ice or high altitudes for soft tissues. Foremost amongst the scientists in the very tricky business of recovering ancient DNA is Svaante Pääbo and his colleagues in the University of Munich.

Pääbo was a student of the late Allan C. Wilson of the University of California, Berkeley, whose lab team recovered the quagga DNA and showed its close, subspecies-level relationship to the zebra. In 1987 Wilson's team developed the 'African Eve' theory for the origin of modern humans. Their global sample of DNA showed so much similarity as to indicate that all modern humans originated from a single African population around 200,000 years ago. Although subsequently criticised for not being statistically significant, further more extensive sampling has verified their basic claims.

Pääbo's Munich team is now working towards improving our understanding of recent human evolution, using ancient DNA. Recently they have found that mitochondrial DNA from the 5,200-year-old 'Ice-man', Otzi, from the Austro-Italian

Alps, is surprisingly close to that of people living in the region today, showing a remarkable genetic stability. Also they have analysed three Neanderthal DNA samples, between 55,000 and 30,000 years old, which turn out to be more similar to one another than to modern European DNA. This suggests that the Neanderthals had a common gene pool that was sufficiently different from that of modern humans to verify their separation as a genuine biological species in their own right. Moreover, it is unlikely that they made any contribution to the modern European gene pool.

Finally, the recent decision to map the chimp genome, which has a 98.8% similarity to our own, promises to give a great boost to the study of human evolution. Examination of that 1% difference between the chimp and the human will perhaps tell us what has differentiated us from the chimps and has turned us into humans. Already there is a strong suggestion that a gene which controls facial muscles related to the production of speech is absent from the chimps. Furthermore, it has been estimated that the appearance of this gene is very recent (within the

last 200,000 years) and is perhaps confined to the species *Homo sapiens*. If this is correct, it will help explain the remarkable success of our species over all other extinct human species, including the Neanderthals.

The rapid evolution of speech would have required significant 'rewiring' of parts of the brain and given a boost to the development of consciousness. Our 'creative spark' has made us so interested in the world around us that we even want to know what happened in the remote geological past. As I tried to show at the beginning of this book, as far as we know no other animal, apart from humans, has ever paid any attention to fossils. The fact that the Neanderthal people were perhaps the first to do so suggests that the taxonomic position of the 'glass floor' to humanness is still debatable. We have come a long way in our understanding of our position in the world. From being one rung below the angels we are now faced with the statistical likelihood that life is not unique to Earth or even our solar system. That does not mean that life and its history on Earth is any less extraordinary and wonderful.

LEFT:
The fossil record can preserve some remarkable aspects of past life. Here, phosphate minerals preserve the 570 million year old fossil embryo of a late Precambrian seacreature with its microscopic (berry-like) cluster of cells

Further reading

Cadbury, Deborah. *The Dinosaur Hunters* (Fourth Estate, 2000)

Currie, Philip J. and Padian, Kevin (eds). *Encyclopedia of Dinosaurs* (Academic Press, 1997)

Dean, Dennis R. *Gideon Mantell and the Discovery of Dinosaurs* (Cambridge University Press, 1999)

Gillispie, Charles C. *Genesis and Geology* (Harper & Row, 1959)

Greene, John C. *The Death of Adam* (Mentor, 1961)

Knell, Simon J. *The Culture of English Geology, 1815–1851* (Ashgate, 2000)

Lister, Adrian and Bahn, Paul. *Mammoths* (Boxtree, 1995)

McGowan, Christopher. *The Dragon Seekers* (Little, Brown, 2002)

Mayor, Adrienne. *The First Fossil Hunters: Paleontology in Greek and Roman Times* (Princeton University Press, 2000)

Novacek, Michael J. *Dinosaurs of the Flaming Cliffs* (Anchor/Doubleday, 1996)

Palmer, D. *The Atlas of the Prehistoric World* (Marshall Publishing, revised edition 2000)

Palmer, D. 'Resurrecting the Mammoth', in Grayson, A. (ed) *Equinox: The Earth* (Channel 4 Books, 2000)

Palmer, Douglas. *Neanderthal* (Channel 4 Books, 2000)

Rudwick, Martin J. S. *The Meaning of Fossils* (Macdonald American Elsevier, 1972)

Rudwick, Martin J. S. *Scenes from Deep Time: Early Pictorial Representation of the Prehistoric World* (University of Chicago Press, 1992)

Schopf, J.W. *Cradle of Life* (Princeton University Press, 1999)

Secord, James A. *Victorian Sensation: The Extraordinary Publication, Reception and Secret Authorship of Vestiges of the Natural History of Creation* (The University of Chicago Press, 2000)

Steinbock, R. T. 'Ichnology of the Connecticut Valley: a vignette of American science in the early nineteenth century', in Gillette, D.D. and Lockley, M.G. (eds) *Dinosaur Tracks and Traces* (Cambridge University Press, 1989)

Thulborn, T. *Dinosaur Tracks* (Chapman and Hall, 1990)

Torrens, Hugh. *The Practice of British Geology, 1750–1850* (Ashgate, 2002)

Winchester, Simon. *The Map that Changed the World: William Smith and the Birth of Modern Geology* (Viking, 2001)

Young, David. *The Discovery of Evolution* (Cambridge University Press, 1992)

Picture Credits

All reasonable efforts have been made by the Publisher to trace the copyright holders of the photographs contained in this publication. In the event that a copyright holder of a photograph has not been traced, but comes forward after the publication of this edition, the Publishers will endeavour to rectify the position at the first possible opportunity.

The positions of the photographs on each page of the book are indicated as follows:
t = top, l = left, c = centre, r = right, b = bottom

Clive Bromhall/Oxford Scientific Films 8, 49;
© N.A.Callow/Robert Harding Picture Library Ltd 9; Cambridge University Museum of Archaeology and Anthropology 10t;
© Chris Henshilwood/National Science Foundation 10b; © John Boardman/Boston Museum of Fine Art 11t; © Jean Vertut 12t; Bolton Museum & Art Gallery 13; © The British Museum 14, 54;
© Adrian Lister 15; © Leicester City Museums Service 23; Swedish library archive 25; © The Royal Society of London 27; St Petersburg Zoological Institute archive 29; © Natuurhistorisch Museum, Maastricht 33; John Martin 36; © The Natural History Museum, London 40, 67, 93t, 96, 137, 138, 139, 258, 259; © Mary Evans Picture Library 49; © Michael Richards/Oxford Scientific Films 49bl; © CIBA, Basle 59; © Bettman/Getty Images 60; © George Richmond/National Portrait Gallery, London 66; © Oxford University Museum of Natural History 92; © Dr P.J. Griffiths 104; California Institute of Technology 111; History of Science Collections, University Libraries, University of Oklahoma 113; University of California, Los Angeles 119; K.M.Towe, The Smithsonian Institute 123; Photographs courtesy of the Smithsonian Institution (Dr D. Erwin), 127; University of Cambridge (H.B. Whittington), 128; © Zhexi Luo, Yuanqing Wang, Yaoming Hu and Chuankui Li/Nature, volume 390, 137-147, 1997 134, 135; © Shuhai Xiao (Tulane University) and Andrew H. Knoll (Harvard University) contents, 140;
© N.K Vereshchagin 142

Acknowledgements

My interest in the history of the earth sciences was originally stimulated many years ago by hearing Professor Martin Rudwick enthuse over the importance of illustration to the development of the subject. Since then I have picked up so many insights and information from hearing other historians of science – such as Professor Hugh Torrens – talk, and from reading their work, that I have lost any accurate knowledge of the original sources of many of the topics dealt with here. Any inaccuracies are entirely my own work, and I hope that the experts will forgive me for making them.

I also wish to thank Katie Piper, Luisa Bondi and Helen Brocklehurst of HarperCollins, and Sue Viccars and Les Dominey of Blackingstone Books, for all their efforts, which have significantly improved the book.

BELOW:
Russian scientists recover a mammoth tusk, tens of thousands of years old, from the Siberian Arctic where the ground is permanently frozen

Index